Bruce Tulloh
Four Million Footsteps

50th Anniversary edition

Contents

Foreword

I knew Bruce Tulloh from being on the same International athletics team going to Jamaica for the Commonwealth Games in 1966. I had admired his endurance and turn of speed in his middle-distance races; running barefoot, as he had since his youth on the sand at Instow beach, he became European 5,000m champion and ran sub-four minutes for the mile. All impressive, but not, in fact, the ideal pedigree to tackle an almost 3,000 mile run! As we lived only three miles from one another and since his wife Sue had been instrumental in having us, 35 years ago, look in the Marlborough area for our home, we remained friends, occasionally running together over the Marlborough Downs.

When Bruce was told that he was being referred to as the original Forrest Gump, running across America, he was indignant, saying, 'but the man was a complete idiot!', to which Bruce's son Clive said, 'Well, Dad...!' However, Bruce was a fine example of Renaissance Man. A Cambridge graduate in science, an international athlete and a man with multiple interests from singing in choirs, loving literature, doing the daily *Guardian* crossword, to enjoying the Goons and word play.

This book is extraordinary. Bruce recalls the long preparation and the struggle to find sponsorship; and once committed to the challenge, we run with him, sharing, as best we can, the feelings and levels of exhaustion, both mentally and physically, to virtually cover a marathon before lunch and another after lunch for more than two months! Injuries had to be dealt with en route, with a record time in mind.

Frequently he mentions the pains and strains that this endeavour occasioned, requiring many miles simply walking in boots, to calm calf or thigh cramps and strains. However, the human body is such a remarkable self-healing entity, he arrived in New York in better condition than he left Los Angles. His mental fortitude is apparent throughout the story, including the continual and often tediously repetitive interviews. Bruce's flippant answer to the question 'Why are you running across America?' was 'To get to the other side!' Lovely!

The journey could not have been completed without his wife Sue. In the era before mobile phones and the internet, she had daily to find an appropriate camp site, drive to pre-arranged stopping places, provide the essential drinks and food in the morning, at lunch time and at tea time, cook a hot meal every evening (the essential fuel for Bruce, who described himself by the end as 'a running machine') and administer foot and calf massages. With the able assistance of cousin Mark, they together drove and supported this epic journey, all the time also looking after seven-year-old Clive, often taking him off on various adventures while Bruce ran on.

Bruce writes well and the reader is given a flavour of the terrain, the people, towns and features in each of the states he traversed. At one point in the recounting of this extraordinary feat, I felt exhausted simply reading about the next and the next running distance of the day. One can only admire the awesome achievement of beating the previous best time by more than six days! It is an interesting and of course a breathtaking read and will be enjoyed by anyone, but especially runners or someone contemplating a serious endurance challenge.

Dr David Hemery, CBE
Olympic Gold Medallist
September 2019

Bruce Tulloh

A running chronology
from birth to the start of the
Transcontinental Run

Born September 29th, 1935, Datchet, Berkshire to Margaret and Tony
Tulloh. As a small baby Bruce was slow to thrive and aged six months
was admitted to a nursing home suffering from malnutrition. He recovered
and spent happy early years in North Devon where his parents rented a
fisherman's cottage in Appledore on the Taw Torridge estuary opposite
the village of Instow. The latter's kilometre-long sandy beach would be the
setting for many of Bruce's barefoot training sessions as a young athlete.

1939
With the outbreak of war Margaret and Bruce moved to live with her
parents in the village of Stonegrave, North Yorkshire. Bruce was a helpful
little boy and spent much time scurrying about on the command of his
grandfather who would demand 'Brucie boy, run upstairs and find my
glasses, would you?' or 'Run and get a few more logs, there's a good boy.'
With petrol rationing there was not much driving about and Bruce and
his mother would go for long walks, pushing his younger brother, Robin
in his pram.

1942
Bruce's first endurance run took place aged seven when he ran away from
school. The prep school was six miles from Stonegrave, in the village of
Helmsley. Out on a Sunday walk with his class Bruce realised he was on
the road home. He mentioned the idea of escaping to his companion who
promptly dared him. Wartime exploits of prisoners of war trying to get
home were partly to blame for this impulse. Bruce set off cross country;

showing the first signs of his future readiness to accept a physical challenge he zigzagged across fields, running along beneath hedges and covering his head with his jacket when he saw soldiers (billeted locally). He made it home only to encounter his mother and younger brother out for a walk. Bruce greeted her with the words 'Mummy, I've run away'. He was returned to school next day where they had failed to notice his absence.

It was a small school and there was no organised running. There were however lots of games of hide-and-seek in the grounds after tea which Bruce won by running further away than anyone else.

1947

With the end of the war the school returned to its original site at Saltburn-by-the-Sea. Here in November Bruce won his first race. 'It was the school cross country—mostly on the road. At twelve, I was one of the older ones. We were running in a group of four or five and when we got past half way, someone said: "Let's stop and walk for a bit." But I said: "No, I'm going on", so I did. As I was useless at other sports, that small achievement stuck in my head—I was a runner.'

1948

Bruce was enrolled at Wellington College in Berkshire where his father had been a foundation scholar. Wellington was originally founded as a school for the sons of deceased military officers and with a strong military ethos, compulsory cadet force and emphasis on rugby it was a poor fit for the quiet, bookish Bruce. He managed to get himself into the back end of the cross country team. Cross country only got one term (Lent) and not many races.

1953

At the end of his final term Bruce received his first sporting disappointment when he failed to receive his school colours for cross country. The fact that they were given to another boy of equal talent whose name, Custance, Bruce recalled with rancour seventy years later, really stung. After failing to get into Cambridge he decided to do his national service before applying to other universities. He travelled to Oswestry, Shropshire to train with the Royal Artillery. Physically a late developer he would grow another two inches whilst in the army.

1954

On May 6th Bruce joined the army. It was the same day that Roger Bannister broke four minutes for the mile at Iffley Road track, Oxford. To an under-sized 18-year-old Bruce this seemed like a magical achievement.

After a few weeks of basic training Bruce was sent to Tonfanau on the Welsh coast where along with the various disciplines peculiar to artillery men such as sound ranging and radar operations there were also regular races, in which Bruce finished second in his intake. He was then sent to Salisbury Plain for Artillery Survey training. As he had put himself down as agnostic, he did not have to attend church on Sundays so instead ran from Larkhill to Stonehenge, round the stones and back. During a race on grass he managed 18 minutes something on a grass track. One night whilst on guard duty he slipped into the TV room to watch the Russian Vladimir Kuts and Britain's Chris Chataway battle it out to set a new world 5,000m world record of 13:52.8 before a crowd of 40,000 at White City. Chataway later called it 'the most extravagant race I have ever run' and the 'most painful quarter mile of my life'. For Bruce it was pure poetry and total inspiration.

In November Bruce was posted to Hong Kong for his national service and sails from Southampton. The journey, by liner, through the Bay of Biscay, Gibraltar, the Mediterranean, the Suez Canal, taking in a visit to Aqaba then on to Aden, Colombo, Singapore and finally Hong Kong. After morning parades and a few lectures there was not much to do so Bruce ran around the deck 'because in my mind I was still a runner'.

1955

As part of 173 Locating Battery, Bruce was stationed on a hill overlooking Shaukiwan Gap, the entrance to Hong Kong harbour. Duties were light, Bruce bought a tiny dinghy with a sampan sail with a Cornish friend and signed up for a Chinese language course. He continued running, racing behind the trams to Shaukiwan back from the city, whose passengers shouted at him. In the trials for the Battery athletic team Bruce was chosen as second string for three miles. In the Land Forces Championships Bruce outsprinted the No. 1 with a time of 16:20 for three miles. Shortly after running in the colours of the Hong Kong Athletic Club Bruce won the Colony 5,000m title. It was a new and giddy height. During this time, he came across *Zatopek in Photographs* in a Communist bookshop, which gave a straightforward account of this great runner's rise to success. He also read a fellow-soldier's copy of *Franz Stamphl on Running* (foreword by Roger Bannister, introduction by Chris Chataway). It became his bible; he reads in the introduction: 'I put little store by the build of a man, and, within certain limits, I am not much influenced by his running style. What does matter is whether he can physically and mentally absorb training in the quantity it takes to be a champion.' Inspired by this, Bruce followed Stamphl's training plan which draws on the work of German coach, Woldemar Gerschler and his system of interval training. A month following the three-mile plan might be:

MONDAY: 20 × 440 yards in 71   TUESDAY: 8 × 880 yards in 2:18
WEDNESDAY: 15 × 440 yards in 69   THURSDAY: 5 × ¾ miles in 3:30
FRIDAY: Gym   SATURDAY: 1 hour fartlek   SUNDAY: Rest

Bruce continued to win races and improve. The following winter he trained six days a week.

1956

By the time he flew home from Hong Kong Bruce was running 4:36 for a mile and 15:46 for three miles. These were good times for a schoolboy athlete, but Bruce was 20. He returned to his mother's tiny cottage in the village of Instow where he spent the summer working as a night porter at the Marine Hotel for £5 a week plus supper. The hours (7 pm to 1 am) gave him plenty of time for training on the beach, the dunes and the maze of hilly country lanes behind the village. He joined Barnstaple Athletic Club whose members met once a week at the rugby club to train on grass. The nearest cinder track was at Plymouth sixty miles away. Running barefoot was partly a matter of circumstance—it is lovely to run barefoot on the sands—and also the influence of the back-to-nature, barefoot running philosophy of Australian running legend Herb Elliot's coach, Percy Cerutty, who had established a coastal training camp at Portsea, Australia. Cerutty's regime involved raw food, poetry and philosophy combined with running in idyllic circumstances which happily for Bruce, Instow also provided.

Running on Instow beach would be a life-long pleasure for Bruce. During the summer Bruce participated in competitions across Devon (handicapped to give novice runners so many yards start against the more experienced); they were amateur competitions with prizes such as lamps, toasters or canteens of cutlery. At the end of the summer his increased leg strength from dune running meant his time was down to close to two minutes for a half mile. At Bideford Regatta Sports (the nearest local town) Bruce gave British International Peter Driver a hard run. Driver was encouraging, believing the youthful looking Bruce to be a schoolboy.

In the autumn Bruce went to Southampton University to study Botany. He joined the cross country team which went on to win the Southern Universities Cup and the UAU cup for smaller universities. Although he was less successful at cross country than track running Bruce saw it as an important part of his training year. 'Cross country running is the best way to build up all-round strength and stamina, while avoiding the high-impact stress of running on the road or the track. It has hills, it has heavy going, it has twists and turns, so it uses all the muscles in the body.' The arrival of a post-graduate student Martin Hyman was significant. The pair raced together and spurred each other on to greater success. In 1958 Bruce was the British Universities Student Champion over three miles but was still a big step away from international competition coming only 16th in his first AAA championship over three miles.

1959

At the start of the track season Bruce representing Devon at an Inter-Counties match at the White City came fifth in the three miles in 13:46, a new and significant personal best. Two days later Martin Hyman won the six miles and Bruce finished 45 seconds later in 29:10, another new personal best. July 11th was the day that changed his life. He had just taken his final exams at Southampton University and was working at the Institute for Agricultural Botany as a gardener. Because of exams he had not been doing much training but had been racing twice a week. He arrived at the White City for the AAA championship with low expectations having finished last the previous year. However, none of the big stars (Gordon Pirie, Derek Ibbotson or Stan Eldon) turned up. Bruce warmed up in jeans and a sailing sweater as his only tracksuit had been stolen and he couldn't afford to buy another.

The White City track built for the 1908 Olympics, was black ash. The three miles was the last race and by the end of the day the surface was pretty churned up, so Bruce stuck on some strips of Elastoplast round the ends of his toes, to help withstand the friction. This is how he described the race: 'The early laps ticked by—4:30 first mile—and at two miles in 9:05 I was still in the leading bunch, feeling comfortable. With a kilometre to go, Peter Clarke streaked into the lead and opened up a gap. No one seemed willing to chase him, so with two laps left I got going. I caught him up just before the bell, expecting a struggle, but he gasped "you go on, Bruce" and let me pass. I ran the next 220 yards as if my life depended on it and held on desperately up the home straight. I won in 13:31.'

'Barefoot hero kicks out the stars!' screamed the *Daily Express* the next morning. Athletics was big news in those days and Bruce became an instant celebrity. He was picked to run against the USSR in the Lenin Stadium in Moscow and finished 2nd in the 5,000m, in 13:55, which put him into the top dozen in the world rankings. He would later say 'the first chance to run for your country is one of the biggest things that will ever happen to you.' He bought himself a new tracksuit and in Moscow a Russian hat (which he wore in cold weather for the rest of his life).

1960

Bruce attended Cambridge University where he took a postgraduate diploma in Agricultural Science at Selwyn College. At the annual Oxford *v* Cambridge athletics match he broke the British record for three miles (13:17.2) and qualified for the Rome Olympics. In hot and humid conditions Bruce finished fourth in his heat for the 5,000m, just missing out on the twelve-man final. During the Christmas vacation Bruce returned to Devon. He met his future wife Susan Baker at the Saunton Golf Club dance and they were married the following year.

1961

Bruce and Sue, now married, moved to Wargrave-on-Thames. Bruce finished third in the Inter-Counties Cross country and then placed second in the National championships. The season of tough cross country running prepared him well for the track season. He rad 39 races between May and September, running 51.5 for 440 yards, 1:53 for 800m and took his mile time down to 4:04 seconds. The one failure was the AAA 5,000m championships—a late downpour saw the cinder track turn to greasy mud;

in bare feet Bruce was unable to stay in touch and dropped out after six laps. A month later at an inter-club meeting at Southampton Bruce broke the British record for three miles again in a time of 13:12, the third-fastest time in history. During this time Bruce continued to work for Shell, who were understanding about his frequent trips abroad, at least while he was winning.

1962

On a tour of New Zealand Bruce ran what he thought of as his best race, the race in which he fought hardest and nearly beat an Olympic champion. It was a two-mile race, the line-up of which included several world class athletes among them Murray Halberg (NZ)—Olympic 5,000m champion and world record holder for two and three miles— and Albie Thomas (Aus)—Commonwealth champion and former world record holder for two and three miles. The small stadium had a crowd of 10,000 people. The final lap saw Bruce and Halberg fighting it out right down to the tape. The pair threw themselves over the line but Halberg had it in a time of 8:33.7 with Bruce just a tenth of a second behind. Both men had set national records. The exhilaration of the last-lap battle is something Bruce always remembered. Three days later at Wanganui Bruce and Halberg were running in a mile event to showcase Peter Snell which was intended to be the first sub-four-minute mile in New Zealand. With 352 yards to go Bruce shot into the lead galvanising Snell who ran the last lap in 55 seconds, setting a new world record of 3:54.5; Bruce ran 3:59.3, becoming the sixth British athlete to break four minutes.

This year Bruce and Sue's son Clive was born on May 24th. That summer Bruce won 19 races out of 20, culminating in the European 5,000m championships in Belgrade. In a particularly gutsy performance Bruce blew apart a slow tactical race; sprinting for home from 700m, he ran his final 800m in 1:59 and his race in a time of 14:00.6. When he went to bed there was a note from his friend and co-competitor Martin Hyman; it read simply 'Good'. Later in the same year Bruce, Clive and Sue flew to Perth, Western Australia for the Commonwealth Games. Despite beating Ron Clarke and Kip Keino in a two mile race before the games Bruce only finished fourth in the three miles behind Murray Halberg, Ron Clarke and a young Kip Keino.

1963

International success meant lots of invitations to run abroad. As an amateur there was no cash involved but the race organisers paid for Sue to go too. Bruce ran in Austria, Finland and Jamaica. September saw him beaten in a GB *v* West Germany match and again by a Swede Sven-Olaf Larrson. He fared better in the GB *v* Russia match in Volgograd, coming in second behind his British teammate in the 5,000m and also unexpectedly stepping in and competing in the 10,000m. These extra points helped Britain to a narrow victory over Russia.

1964

The track season started well, with a three mile Inter-Counties win at White City in a time of 13:23. With the Olympics in sight, Bruce trained harder than ever but contracted measles and never fuller recovered his form. He had overtrained and failed to qualify for the Tokyo Olympics. He was bitterly disappointed.

1965

At the AAA three miles championship Ron Clarke ran 12:52, demolishing ideas about what a good time for three miles was; Bruce came in 13th. Work had always come second place to running so it was no real surprise when Bruce was called in to Shell head office and given the sack. Bruce decided to start looking for a job in teaching. He was 30 and would have to train a lot harder to stay in the top class. He upped his mileage, almost doubling his average from a year before from 200 to 400 miles a month. He took a job at Dr Challoner's Grammar School in Amersham which was particularly strong in sport. The job meant a drop in pay but more support from the school and longer holidays.

1966

The 65/66 winter season went well and at Whitsun Bruce won the Inter-Counties six miles in just over 28 minutes. He was back in the British team running against the USSR at White City. Bruce came second to the Russian Gennady Klistov in a new personal best of 28:50. At the AAA 10,000m championships Bruce ran a tough race but was just beaten by the Tunisian, Mohammed Gammoudi; nevertheless he had set a new British record of 27:23.78; he felt it had been the toughest race of his life. He went to Jamaica for the Commonwealth Games but pulled a muscle training and was unable to compete. In the end the race was blown away by the Kenyan, Neftali Temu, who won in 27:14, lapping everyone except for the world record holder Ron Clarke. Bruce did run in the three miles but only came 14th. Three weeks later Bruce was in Budapest running in the 10,000m. The race was won in 28:26, nowhere near the time Bruce had run at the AAA. In the end Bruce was sixth in 28:50, leaving him to question whether his trip to Jamaica had cost him a European title. The Mexico Olympics were two years away; they would be held in Mexico City at 7,500ft Bruce knew he had no chance of winning unless he could spend time at altitude. With no realistic way of doing this and supporting a family he decided to finish his international career at the end of the 1967 track season. He had spent eight years as an international and had broken the two-mile, three-mile and six-mile British records.

1967

Although planning to retire Bruce continued to train hard and won a sixth Inter-Counties six-mile title in a championship record of 27:42. It was his best race of the season and was picked to represent the Commonwealth against the USA in Los Angeles. As part of an experiment into the effects of altitude training (in the run up to the Mexico Olympics) the British Board had sent six runners to train in Mexico. For the group's final time trial Bruce took part, winning in a time of 13:12.6, just six tenths outside his best ever, set over six years ago. He was 32. In nine years as a GB and England international he had 53 overseas races. On the track he had about thirty international selections as well as one Olympic Games, two Commonwealth Games and two European Championships. At cross country he had 22 overseas races. He visited every country in Western Europe, as well as Russia, Poland, Israel, Algeria, Yugoslavia and Hungary, and also competed in Japan, Australia, New Zealand, Jamaica and the USA and had just started a new job at a comprehensive school outside Reading.

Bruce finished his amateur career on a high. He settled into his new teaching routine but soon began to think of a new challenge: setting a new record for running across America. This book is the story of that run.

Preface

This is a personal story of my journey across the United States. My comments are purely the results of my own experiences; they are inspired by no other motive than that of enlightening the reader. Although references will be found in the text to the various firms and individuals who helped us, I would like to acknowledge their assistance at the start. Many adventures such as mine depend on the imagination and active encouragement of commercial organisations, and it would be churlish not to give them their due, for without them the world would be a duller place.

I would like to thank Schweppes (USA) Inc. and Pan American Airways for covering the expenses of our travel, British Leyland Motors Inc. and Caravans International for the loan of the cars and caravan respectively, *The Observer* and Thames Television, who by paying for the material they received made the trip financially viable, and the makers of Adidas Shoes, Walton's Tufsox and Elliman's Athletic Rub, whose products literally kept me on my feet during those 65 memorable days. Lastly and most importantly I would like to thank my many friends, both in Britain and the United States, whose support and encouragement helped the enterprise to a successful conclusion.

Bruce Tulloh
September 1969

The Runner

On a flat road runs the well-train'd runner,
He is lean and sinewy with muscular legs,
He is thinly clothed, he leans forward as he runs,
With lightly closed fists and arms partially raised.

Walt Whitman

Chapter 1
The Arrival

On the morning of June 25th, 1969, I lay in bed listening to the rain. I had slept in many different places in the last three months, and it took me a moment to recollect where I was. I was in a motel, beside an expressway. The motel was just north of Perth Amboy, in the State of New Jersey, and it was 20 miles from New York. Behind me lay over nine weeks of continuous running and walking, all the way across the North American continent from Los Angeles on the Pacific coast. Those nine weeks contained many days of sweat and toil, sometimes even pain; all I had to do now was run 20 miles, in order to set a new record for the world's longest run.

There wasn't time to lie in bed for long, I woke up my wife Sue; we dressed quickly and piled the last of our things into the already heaped-up suitcases. For the last time I put on my running kit—yellow t-shirt and shorts, yellow sweater and track trousers. In the other bed the only sign of our son Clive was a little bit of blond hair above the bedclothes, so we left him and went for breakfast. Like all American breakfasts, it was both quickly served and good to eat—fresh orange juice, scrambled eggs and crispy bacon, toast and honey and fresh coffee.

Although it was only seven o'clock there was already one newspaper reporter in the breakfast-room waiting for me, and a radio station rang up to record an interview, but we'd got used to that by now. My cousin Mark shambled into the room, looking rather sleepy—he is over six feet, well built and strongly tanned, with long curly hair and a beard. While he finished breakfast, I got ready to go, and at five to eight Maury Soward, our PR man, drove me the mile or so down to my starting point, followed by a press car.

Last night's run had finished up in a place called Fords, at the junction of Amboy Avenue and King George Street; it was essential that I started again from the exact point. The newspaper man was going to run with me for the first mile to get his story, so I set off at a fairly gentle pace, especially as the traffic was thick. The rain had eased off but there was still a damp mist. The streets, the cars, the sky, all appeared in various shades of grey. It was very different from those bright mornings in the West, with the crickets singing and the sky implacably blue. When the reporter left me and I was on my own it was hard to think that this was different from just any morning run, apart from being wetter than usual.

The streams of traffic carrying commuters to work did not notice me. I had studied the route on the map the night before—it was Route 440 most of the way, which first cut across the maze of construction and expressways, and then became very quiet as it approached the Outerbridge Crossing, the bridge which connects Perth Amboy to Staten Island. There was very little traffic on the approach to the bridge—a long curve of concrete. I passed a crossing patrol lady, clad in yellow plastic against the rain. She stared in disbelief as I padded down the road towards the bridge, then shouted after me, 'You can't run there! You can't cross there.' I hadn't got the time to stop and explain it all to her, so I just waved and kept on running, but not for long. Before I reached the bridge, a yellow police car slid alongside me. The cop gave me a hard look and jerked his thumb. 'Off, buddy,' he said, 'can't you read?' I felt a bit worried, but I went over and explained to him that I had run all the way from Los Angeles, and that I was due at City Hall at noon, to meet the Mayor. His reaction was what I expected: he gave a big grin and told me to be careful of the traffic, but he took my name and address, just in case.

Crossing the Outerbridge took me into New York State. On the New York side was the toll office, where I was greeted by a rather striking Jewish lady in a pink uniform. 'Ya got some money for me?' I said I hadn't. 'Ya run from California? Ya mus' be crazy.' I agreed that I was, and English as well, so she let me go.

Staten Island is one of the world's most heavily populated areas, so there must be a reason for its being largely uninhabited, but I don't know what it is. I had a quiet run along a wide road, with trees and bushes either side and practically no traffic. I came to some construction work and got red mud all over the new running shoes I had put on that morning. At about nine o'clock my cavalcade rolled past—Maury in his Volkswagen camper, Sue in her little brown Austin with Clive, Mark in the white MGB, towing the trailer and the press car that had come out earlier on. When they stopped to check the route with me it made quite a sight, and within a couple of minutes a police car had arrived, to see if there had been a crash or a breakdown.

The road wound on, becoming a bit more built up, with the smell of mud and salt marsh drifting in from the estuary. We stopped beside a derelict café, to give me a rest before the last stage, and to give Sue and Mark a chance to put on their smart clothes. The photographer took some more shots, then just after ten I set off again. It was seven miles to the ferry which would take us across the harbour to Manhattan, and it was due to leave at 11.10.

The rain came down again, the troupe drove on past me and I was alone again. Only a handful of miles now, and it still seemed unlikely that this was really the end. I couldn't get excited, it seemed a long seven miles, mostly through rather a scruffy dockland area, nobody gave me a second look. When I was on the last mile or so, downhill to the ferry terminal, then I allowed myself to feel a glow of satisfaction, but after that it was too hectic to feel anything but confused.

At the ferry terminal I ran towards the pedestrian entrance; there was a single photographer there, and he led me through to the turnstiles. It is only a nickel to ride on the Staten Island ferry—they say it's the best value for money in New York, and I'd agree. There were two or three English reporters in the entrance hall, and I talked to them while we waited for the gates to open—it was only eleven o'clock. There didn't seem to be many TV people about, which was odd, as I knew that Schweppes had got everything organised. I walked on to the ferry, then went down to the car deck, expecting to find Sue and the vehicles. Nobody there. I walked out to the car entrance and bedlam broke loose. The cars and caravan were still on shore, waiting for me to arrive! They were surrounded by a 50-strong horde of newsmen, and the ferry was due to leave!

The newsmen ran towards me, I ran towards the cars, Sue, Mark and Maury jumped into the cars and we all rushed on to the ferry, where they were holding the centre lane for us. Confusion increased as the cameramen had to get on first to film me coming on. The moment we were on board the ferry set out, and it seemed to be tearing through the choppy grey water of the harbour, though in fact it takes half an hour for the. four-mile journey.

Of all the various forms of media, the photographers are the most aggressive, and the New York photographers are known to be the most extreme of their breed. They pranced around us like cannibals round a juicy captive, turning us this way and that, as we stood up in the bows, Sue beside me and Clive between us. 'Look at me, Bruce.' 'Look at your husband, lady.' 'Now point out to sea.' 'Let's have the little boy up on your shoulders.' 'Look at me.' 'Turn your face.' 'Would you look up, please?'

Then it was the turn of the TV interviewers, who almost came to blows with the photographers. We'd promised Thames Television in England that we'd do the first interview for them, but it was a job finding which of the three crews was filming for Thames, and when we declined to be interviewed by one man, he really turned quite unpleasant.

However, nothing could spoil this moment for us. The Statue of Liberty loomed up out of the greyness, and then the towering skyscrapers of Manhattan. The shapes of both are so familiar from pictures that they have become symbols as much as real objects. Here they came into our view like familiar, welcoming giants. The wind and spray blew in our faces; Sue's eyes sparkled and her face glowed; Clive shouted and pointed. The news people continued to film and ask questions, and so we came to New York.

Outside the ferry terminal a police car was waiting to escort me up to City Hall. The reporters crowded after us, two of them wearing shorts to run with me, and the photographers started to run ahead. I was getting a bit impatient of all this, so I asked the police car not to hang around. Owing to the continual construction work, the route was not completely straight. I went on behind the escort, with my two self-appointed running companions alongside, and a load of photographers in Maury's camper just behind me.

After 100 yards I started to speed up, and after another 100 yards my running mates dropped back. I had no objection to them personally, they were only doing their job, but after doing most of the 2,875 miles on my own, I felt entitled to have the last mile to myself. The photographers drove in front of me to get their pictures, and just behind, two cars with TV cameramen on them jostled for position like chariots. I ran faster and faster. The lights were held for us; people in the streets stopped to look; gusts of steam blew up from the manhole covers. The hundreds of weary hours dropped from my feet as I covered the last quarter of a mile, veered across the square on my left and jogged up the steps of City Hall.

The clock stood at ten minutes to noon. I had covered the distance from City Hall Los Angeles, 2,876 miles, on foot, in 64 days, 21 hours and 50 minutes. I had improved on the previous fastest crossing by eight-and-a-half days, averaging over 44 miles a day.

So what? Was there any value in all this effort? Was there any point? What did it mean to me to have done it? These are questions that cannot be answered briefly, but I hope that the answers will appear during the course of the succeeding chapters.

Chapter 2
The idea and the reality

The idea for the run came in November 1967. Two young athletes from Reading Athletic Club, Paul Lightfoot and Ron MacAndrew, had come over to my house for a training session. After training we had supper and then sat over our coffee talking about runners and running. Ron and Paul had been on the Reading AC relay from Land's End to John O'Groats, covering the whole length of Britain—860 miles at 10 mph pace, with a ten-man team.

Among other things the talk got around to the great Wilson, a fictional athlete who has over the years exerted a powerful influence on readers of the boys' comic *Wizard*. Wilson, a slim ageless figure wearing black running kit, did the seven-foot high jump, the 27-foot long jump and the four-minute mile years ahead of real athletes, and although his marks in these events have been improved upon in real life, they still had a magic quality about them. It was his feats of endurance, however, which made the most profound impression. He was apt to slip away after an international track meeting in London and return to his native Yorkshire moors on foot, covering the 200 miles in little more than a day, with his tireless jog-trot. In his outward appearance he was unimpressive, with his rough tweed suit and rather heavy shoes—doubtless a comforting thought to many of his awkward schoolboy followers—but when he started running you could be sure that his opponents were in for a defeat of the most traumatic kind. Many of his greatest achievements were done purely for his own satisfaction, away from any audience, pitting himself against some legendary figure of the past, and it was by the merest coincidence that his faithful scribe happened to be on hand to record his exploits for the benefit of the readers of the *Wizard*.

A day or two after this discussion, Ron MacAndrew brought over to my house the current edition of *The Guinness Book of Records*, which has everything in it from the lightest gas to the biggest known mammal, and naturally includes a section on running records. In this I found the record set by Don Shepherd of South Africa, who in 1964 covered the distance from Los Angeles to New York, 3,200 miles, in 73 days and eight hours. The thought struck me immediately that this would be a good record to go for. I took the book in to Sue, who was in the kitchen, read her the record and said: 'that'd be a good one to have a go at. What do you think?' She said: 'Yes, darling, it sounds fun', and went on getting supper. I don't know whether she thought I was serious or not, but from that moment the idea was in my mind.

The more I thought, the more good reasons there seemed to be for doing it. I hadn't been out of the country since I got back from Poland at the end of August, and with no more amateur running in front of me heaven knows when the next chance would be. Sue hadn't been on a trip since going to Budapest and back by car in 1966, and Clive had never been abroad, or on a plane, and frequently reminded me of the fact. This would be a trip on which we could all go; I couldn't contemplate doing it without a support group, and Sue was the obvious first choice. Quite apart from being the girl I love, she is a person of all-round competence—a good driver, a good cook, a good secretary, good at handling people, an experienced athlete and an optimist. If we were both going away to America for three months, we had to take Clive with us. It might have been easier for us to leave him behind, but that's not the way we look at things. We have always tried to treat him as a responsible member of the family unit, and to explain our actions and decisions to him as far as possible; not to trust him with sharing this adventure would have been a terrible disappointment, leaving aside the positive benefits which would obviously accrue.

The next attractive feature was the prospect of making money by running. Doing this as a professional would enable me to take on sponsorship and advertising, which under Olympic rules had been forbidden to me in my days as a track runner. Life as a teacher is interesting and rewarding spiritually, but not financially, so this seemed a good way to make a bit extra, using the fitness and know-how which I had accumulated in the previous 13 years.

To help us think about it, I got a large map of the United States and stuck it on the wall. The idea seemed better and better; there were all those exciting names like Forth Worth and Phoenix, Los Angeles and Las Vegas, the Blankburgs and the Dashvilles, each with the promise of unknown sights and unknown people. There was the romantic notion of a country so large and so new that it seemed to have been divided up with a map, a ruler and a magnificent disregard of physical features. I studied one or two hypothetical routes and made enquiries about heights of mountain passes and temperatures. These presented intriguing challenges, both the obvious physical one of doing something tough, and the subtler, satisfying mental ones of planning and thinking your way around difficulties, before they occur.

Around Christmas and the New Year friends tend to drop in, and the map became a good conversation piece, I would mention casually that I was thinking of running across, and my friends would make suitable sounds. Then they'd ask me when I was going to start. This meant going into the matter more thoroughly, and the answer came out that April was the best time to start, and since April 1968 was too close, April 1969 became the nominal date; it was a comfortably long way away. As the summer term runs from mid-April to mid-July, I would have to miss a whole term of school, but that would leave me the whole of the summer holidays, seven or eight weeks, to recuperate if necessary. However, although a break from routine sounded exciting, it required an important moral and financial decision to leave school for one-third of the school year, a decision which could not be made until I was firmly convinced in my own mind that attempting to beat the transcontinental record was both possible and justified. Whether such a thing is justified I leave to the readers of this narrative to decide; I devoted a good deal of time to its possibility, and thereby learnt a lot.

I was lucky in having for a fairly near neighbour a man who has been for many years a bastion of long-distance running in Britain and the world over—John Jewell, the secretary of the Road Runners Club. John is a man who has devoted years to the sport and knows everyone in it, so he was the obvious man from whom to enquire for some more facts. It was from him I learned of the races of 1928 and 1929. It was incredible to me when I first heard about it that over 40 years ago, with the conditions of American roads and the lack of knowledge about long-distance training, that anyone should have contemplated such a race. After I had crossed the continent myself, over much the same route but much better surfaces, it seemed even more incredible.

For my sources of information, I went first to the book *Running in Three Continents*, by the great runner Arthur Newton. There was a man whose factual story is as impressive in its way as Wilson's fictional one. A farmer in South Africa, English-born, Newton was forced off his land mainly by political pressures and took up running at the remarkably late age of 37 as a means of focusing attention on his unjust treatment. This is what he claimed, but I have a suspicion that the flames of athletic ambition burned pretty strongly in him. The combination of ambition, great natural gifts of endurance and the first 'modern' type of training programme, in the sense of both quantity and logical progression, brought him the fame he needed, when he broke first South African, then world long-distance running records. In the 1928 transcontinental race he was in his late forties and nearly at the end of his career, though he did set a world 100-mile record in his fifty-first year. His book gives an excellent idea of what running this ultra-long race was like, but I was able to go one better, and get the story straight from a man who had done it.

I first met Pete Gavuzzi while watching the London to Brighton 54-mile race. When he heard what I was planning he invited me back to his bed-sitter in Ruislip. It was in a dim suburban area, in a group of dull houses, where I found the abode of this amazing man. He was the same size as me, small and chirpy, sounding a typical Cockney, though in fact he was of Italian-French parentage, and had been brought up in Southampton. In 1928 he had been asked to go over to the States by his godfather, who had been a good long-distance man, and was tempted by the reported offer of 25,000 dollars first prize for a race from Los Angeles to New York. Young Gavuzzi, then 21, had been winning some mile and other short races, and it was thought that he might pick up some stage prizes, as well as providing company for Charlie Herst, who was going for the main prize.

'I took it very easy the first few days, the blokes up the front were racing it out every day, but I wasn't worried—I wasn't expected to do anything, you see. I just ambled along at the back with a few other chaps, we'd laugh and talk and play the banjo, and come in hours after the leaders.' Without realising it, Gavuzzi had found the best possible way of getting used to the unique problems of all-day running. After a week, old Charlie dropped out, and young Pete was sent instructions to move up. The leaders had weakened themselves severely by starting too fast, and within a week he had gone into the lead, which he held for 2,000 miles, before having to retire with bad teeth. The following year he had come back as one of the stars and dominated the race the whole way. He had a large book of cuttings which he leafed through as he told me the story.

'Me and Newton got ourselves well prepared for this. We had a truck with beds and all, and a good man to look after us.'

In spite of the $300 entry fee and the fact that they had to pay their own expenses, there was an entry of about 100 for this, the second and last 'Annual Transcontinental Foot Race'. As well as many well-known European runners there were a variety of Americans, including African Americans and Native American Indians. It did not include the winner of the 1928 race, young Andy Payne, who had taken his money and retired. The race was in 79 daily stages, with the time for each stage being added on to the previous times.

'You 'ad to watch these people. Course you knew who your rivals were—the people within a few hours of you—and if one of those made a break you just had to stick near them. Often, I'd be up in front, with Sale's car watching me, and my car'd be back with him, giving him drinks and suchlike, seeing how he was doing.'

Not all were sportsmanlike—some would steal rides on cars to catch up a few hours, while others would go so far as to drain off a rival's water tank, forcing his support car to go back—but as they progressed, they became whittled down to a bunch of very hard men.

'Some o' them stages were very long, over 60 miles, and sometimes you couldn't get a drink between waterholes in the desert, and when you got there you had to bargain with the Indians.'

As they approached the end there were only two men in it, Gavuzzi and the Finnish American, Johnny Salo. The finish was black comedy. Gavuzzi, who held several hours advantage, was persuaded to ease up, so as to make a race of it, the promoter, old C.C. Pyle, was anxious to get a good gate in Los Angeles, to recoup his losses. When they came to the last stage, Gavuzzi had about seven minute lead.

'The last stage was a marathon, you see, being round the track at Willis field. They told us the race would start when we got down there, so I didn't hurry meself. There was this big crowd, you see, and I had to have four men round me to stop meself getting pushed about. We just took it easy, and we stopped for a couple of minutes to let this freight train cross the street. It was going so slow I could have hopped over it, but I wasn't in no hurry, you see.'

When he got down to Willis Field, the race had started, and his precious lead had vanished. Salo ran like a man inspired, and lapped Gavuzzi, but then the Englishman began to gain. He regained the lap he had lost and had to lap the Finn once more to win. Amid great excitement, Salo held on, and after 3,500 miles, after 79 days of running, Gavuzzi was cheated out of his victory by a minute.

It didn't make any difference. Pyle was bankrupt; the income tax officials impounded all the gate money, and none of the runners ever saw a penny of it. Pete Gavuzzi showed me his worthless cheque; it must have been heartbreaking, but he was young, and big enough to take it. Even now, 40 years later, it was possible to understand what he had gone through and share the pride in the achievement that was his. Johnny Salo, a policeman, was killed in an accident at a baseball park two years later. If he had got his money, he would probably be alive today.

As the winter moved slowly towards spring, and there began to be a little daylight time after school, my mind started to grapple with the problems of ways and means. The first problem was to make the scheme financially possible and the second one, to me much smaller, was to get myself fit enough to do it. I figured that it was the kind of thing for which sponsorship worth be forthcoming if I tried hard enough, I reasoned that the United States is a huge market, that firms need publicity and that my run would get publicity. After talking the idea over with a few friends in the worlds of business and communication and receiving a favourable response, we decided to launch the enterprise in style with a dinner in London, a year before the intended start. Sue and I enjoy good dinners anyway, and this was a better excuse than most.

On April 10th, 1968, a small party dined at the Club dell'Arethusa, in the King's Road, Chelsea. The Arethusa had not at that time been open very long and Mimmo Parlanti, himself a keen sportsman, did us well even by his high standards. As I still have one of the menu cards, drawn by Enzo Apicella in the shape of a foot, it is no effort to set down the meal. The guests were all friends of ours, which always makes for a pleasant occasion; two were in the newspaper world, one in television and two were directors of firms who were favourably disposed towards the idea. As we ate our way through melon with Parma ham and the famous green baked lasagne followed by chicken surprise and a special rum baba, washed down by Orvieto, Valpolicella and Asti Spumante, we became less separate representatives of different worlds and more a group, united on a similar level, sharing experience and pleasure and thereby becoming a little bit larger than each would have been on his own. After the coffee and the cognac it disintegrated—some danced, some talked, some left; it is incidental that hardly any of those present actually played a part in the run itself. From that date onwards the die was cast; I had committed myself to going.

There were still many things to be done, but one thing could now be got under way, my training programme. Based on a start date of April 1969 I had twelve months. I reckoned that starting heavy training in September would suffice, giving me seven months of that as long as I remained clear of injury. I therefore had to be fit to take heavy training by the end of August, which meant building up steadily from the beginning of July. In May and June, with quite a pressure of school work, I would content myself with maintaining a state of basic all-round fitness. I've mentioned the 13 years of background training, these were my bank reserves, so to speak. I intended to consolidate these and then to build up, by running gradually increasing distances, an immense 'current account' of endurance training, in preparation for the prolonged and intense 'withdrawal' which I expected to take place in April 1969.

I am basically a lazy man. I don't like to do more than is really necessary. I sized up the problem in front of me by measuring the distance on the map. Different atlases gave different figures, ranging from 2,830 miles to 2,915. Obviously, it depended on which of various alternative routes one chose. My friend David MacJannet, who was hoping to accompany us, measured out the shortest possible route on the Rand McNally atlas. The US Travel Service in London let us have a whole series of State road maps, and we checked and checked the various routes. The figure arrived at was 2,830 miles, although later I revised this to around 2,845, and as we shall see, when we came to do it over the ground rather than over the map, a few more miles crept in. 2,830 looked a lot better than the 3,200 which Shepherd was supposed to have run and this made my job a lot easier.

Whenever I run, I like to have a target—maybe this limits me, but it also helps me, once I have convinced myself that the target is possible. Bearing in mind that I was going to take a shorter route and I still can't figure out why Shepherd ran 300 miles too far—I reckoned that a week was a good chunk to try and knock off the record. This would mean a target of 66 days, a nice memorable figure, especially as I would be on Route 66 for a long way. Sixty-six into 2,830 gives 43 miles a day, so to allow a little margin for error I decided to think in terms of 45 miles a day. This was the goal. Visualise to yourself a place 40 or 50 miles away from you; imagine going there on foot in a day. This would be possible for the average person in a day—indeed it is often done by people in Britain taking part in fund-raising walks for charity—but would you be able to get back on foot the next day? It is unlikely, because your body would set up a violent reaction to the unaccustomed demands made on it, muscles would be stiff, joints would swell up and your feet would probably be swollen and blistered. Imagine trying to go back and forth on this journey every day for ten weeks and you have an idea of what I was taking on.

Being already an experienced runner gave me several advantages but covering this sort of distance every day was as novel to me as it would be to anybody else. I had to use my experience to work out the best kind of preparation in the time available to me. I had never run more than 23 miles at a stretch before, my normal amount of daily training was ten to 15 miles. On the credit side was the fact that the pace required was well within my capabilities, my normal speed on long training runs was about 10 mph (six-minute miles) and in races I would run at around 12 mph (five-minute miles) on the road, and a good deal faster in track races. From the information I had gathered from Newton's book and from Pete Gavuzzi it was clear that 7 or 8 mph was a sensible pace for all-day running. I decided to aim for a 9 mph pace, which would in theory entail only five hours actual running per day to achieve my 45 miles. I was to learn by bitter experience how far apart theory and practice can be!

Training in the summer term was fun. I did a lighter version of my former track training, whenever time allowed. Sometimes I would run ten quarter-miles in 67 seconds each, with a minute's rest in between. Sometimes I would run five or six miles round the playing fields, alternating fast running and jogging. Occasionally I would do a 15-mile run or spend a Sunday morning orienteering—nothing that wasn't well within my powers. I ran a 4:25 mile and 9:30 two miles on one afternoon, so I was obviously retaining a reasonable degree of speed—quite enough for this purpose.

At Whitsun we went for a holiday on Lundy Island with some of our family and friends, and in the intervals of a lot of walking and beer-drinking I managed to improve by three minutes the record for running from the North Light to the South Light—a distance of just over three miles, plus about 150 steps at each end. It was a long way from running from coast to coast, but it was a start.

In the summer holidays I started to impose a bit of self-discipline, running nearly every day and trying to total 70 miles of running a week. Ten miles a day was not hard, especially split up into two sessions, and after two weeks I increased to 80 miles. Running is a pleasure to me and has become over the years a way of life. To carry out a training programme does not mean abandoning other activities, and that summer was a full and happy one. We spent most of it at the seaside in Devon, staying at my mother's cottage. Sometimes I would spend the afternoon prawning in the rocks with Clive, sometimes running on the beach while the others sunbathed. Often, if we were going out somewhere, I would take my running kit and run home afterwards.

One day I decided to run from my mother's cottage at Instow to Sue's parents' beach hut at Croyde—a distance of 16 miles. It was the day of the Air Show at the Chivenor Air Force Base, besides being a Saturday, when all the holidaymakers are changing lodgings; I ran the distance comfortably in an hour and three-quarters, which was exactly the time it took Sue to get over by car!

Three days later my training took a sudden upward leap. I had a telephone call from my friend Derek Ibbotson, who was supposed to be starting on a 180-mile run along the south coast of England as a promotion for a coal firm. The day before it was due to start, he had pulled a muscle, so he was in a spot. The run was broken up into seven daily stages of 25 to 30 miles each, and although there was no time limit, he had been hoping to improve on the time he had taken for the same run in the Easter holiday. I couldn't reach Kent until that evening, so it was decided that Derek's wife Madeleine would do the first day's run. This wasn't quite as cruel as it sounds, because Madeleine is a very good runner, a British international at 800 metres and a former National cross country champion. Nevertheless, 26 miles is a long way and she was very glad when I turned up at Ashford station the following morning, having taken a sleeper up from Devon to London, breakfasted in luxury at the Charing Cross Hotel and taken another train down to Kent. That day and the two succeeding ones I ran 30 miles, mostly in short stages of five miles or so each. At every stop a loudspeaker van would announce my presence, a small crowd would gather, and I would sign a few autographs. This was all very flattering, but the trouble was that during the stops I would stiffen up and suffer painful muscle twinges when I started again. Anyway, I managed 90 miles of this, by which time Derek had recovered enough to take over. I had only been running seriously for three weeks, so it was encouraging, especially as I managed to average a six-minute mile pace practically the whole way. It was my first taste of all-day running, of keeping on the move, never eating two meals in the same place, and I enjoyed it, but this was only for three days, with plenty of support and good hotels to stay in. I could hardly expect hot baths, English breakfasts and room service when I got into the Wild West.

The summer routine continued, with prawning, walking, drinks in little seaside pubs and family dinners with plenty of wine and laughter. Soon it was back to school, and on to the serious training regime. I had got up to 80 miles a week, but I had to prepare myself to run 300 miles a week. It would have been crazy to try to run this distance as well as carrying on with my work, so I decided to tackle the problem in two ways. On the one hand I would try and build up my daily training as far as possible without interfering with my school work; on the other hand, I would start a programme of long runs, 40 to 50 miles, spread over weekends and holidays. My weekly target started off at 100 miles a week, which meant doing 60 miles between Monday and Friday, and 40 miles on Saturday and Sunday. On Monday morning Sue would take me in to school, with my school work and my running kit. I would run the five miles home in the evening; on Tuesday, Wednesday and Thursday I would run both ways, and on Fridays only in to school, being collected in the afternoon. This gave me a steady 40 miles. Twice a week I would go out after school with my school cross country teams and once a week I had a two-hour games period followed by the lunch hour, which enabled me to total up the extra 20 miles.

After two weeks I aimed for 110 miles, in October 120 miles, November 130 to 140, and over the Christmas holidays I tried to achieve 150 miles a week. It was not often that I achieved the full week's target; if we had a meeting at school, or I had to go to London in the evening, then I would have to miss a session, and there was no available time to catch up on it. In order to do 150 miles in a week I had to do my eight sessions to and from school, totalling 40 miles, 15 miles on Thursday mornings—my games day, a 10-mile run after getting back from school on every other day, and a total of 55 miles on Saturday and Sunday. By the time I had finished work at school and run home it would be 6 pm, I usually had a cup of tea and a sandwich before setting out on my 10-mile jog, and I would sit down to supper about eight o'clock. This left me a couple of hours, between nine and eleven, to write the letters to firms, potential sponsors, newspapers, friends in America and do all the other preparatory work. Luckily my years of track training had inured me to this kind of discipline, but even so it got tiresome at times. The fact that I trained at about 10 mph meant that I could get my longest run, about 25 miles, done on a Sunday morning in two-and-a-half hours, giving us time for a glass of beer in the pub before lunch.

It was during this time that I heard from Ted Corbitt, the doyen of American road runners, some more facts about Don Shepherd and his record. They were facts that impressed me tremendously. Shepherd had achieved his ambition to run across the United States of America at the age of 48. This in itself was not so amazing, because he had a long history of participation in ultra-long-distance races behind him, and I knew well that the powers of endurance in a fit man are as great in the forties as at any time in his life. What was amazing was that he had done the trip entirely on his own.

Having saved up enough for his fare and ten dollars a day expenses, he had sailed from South Africa to New York, and then taken a Greyhound bus to Los Angeles. During this time, he was unable to train, and therefore started out below his maximum fitness. He carried with him a small canvas bag, covered in foam rubber to prevent friction, and containing washing kit, plastic mac, travellers' cheques, maps, water bottle and a kit for gluing fresh rubber to the soles of his shoes. Each day he would set off eastwards, over unknown territory, relying on his own ability to reach a motel or a village before nightfall. Many people gave him help along the way, but he was often hungry and thirsty before he reached the end of his day's journey, and before he reached New York he had acquired several injuries and lost 33 pounds in weight. It was a story of remarkable courage, and though I set out to beat his time, it was done in a spirit not of rivalry but of emulation. It was the thought of his great effort that spurred me on during that winter of training.

I don't want to give the impression, though, that all this meant a tremendous sacrifice for either of us. My philosophy is that sport, even on this level, should add to your life rather than diminish it. There were a good few times when I would cut down on or miss a training session to go out with Sue, to see a film or to visit friends. The long weekend runs had to be fitted in with our overall plans for the weekend, and the result was that the weekly mileage tended to be a bit up and down rather than a steady upward climb. This did not bother me very much, because the training is not important in itself, but only its end result, that of being well prepared and eager to go at the right time. My physical state I could judge by my performance on the planned long runs. In the summer I had found a single 20-mile run to be quite tiring. In the summer holidays I managed that 90 miles in three days but was stiff for a week after it.

In October I tried my first 45-mile day. I ran my five-mile circuit through the woods before breakfast, then went out again at ten o'clock and ran 20 miles, taking it easily, in two-and-a-quarter hours. So far, so good, but this was little more than my normal Sunday morning routine. I gave myself a good long siesta after lunch, and at 3.15 pm set off on my 15-mile run. The expected stiffness did not develop; I covered it in 1 hour 35 minutes, and at 6 pm, after tea, I managed a further five miles in 40 minutes. The next day I was able to fall into my normal weekday training routine, so I felt happy that my work was bringing the required result. I did several more 20 to 30-mile weekend runs and did another 40-mile day in November. The next step was to try successive days of long running, so at the beginning of December I decided to spend the weekend running to Bristol, a distance of 84 miles. The problem here was to get the necessary amount of food and rest on the open road. It is one thing running 45 miles in a day from your own home, with hot baths, good meals and space to lie about in, but quite another to do it in winter on a major highway, with only a small car accompanying you.

It was not possible to have many stopping places, without running to a lot of expense, so I settled for booking in at a hotel for lunch on each day and in another hotel on the Saturday night. Sue had a slightly embarrassing time ringing up the hotels and booking a bedroom for two hours in the middle of the day! Eventually she convinced them that it was a special case, and that we were not a pair of clandestine lovers bent on adultery in the afternoon. Anyway, we found three nice old English inns, the Chequers at Newbury, the Sun at Marlborough and the Angel at Chippenham. The combination of cold weather and only one stop a day made the run pretty hard. The first 24 miles into Newbury was normally tiring, the afternoon 20 got harder towards the end, next morning's 22 was hard because I was stiff as well as cold, and the last 18, including quite a bit of rise and fall, I found very painful indeed, and slowed considerably from the 9 mph pace I had kept up the rest of the way. At that time, I would have had a real struggle to do another full day, but by the time I tried the next long one my body had gone some way towards making the necessary adjustments. This was a run to Exeter, where Sue's parents live, a distance of 140 miles from home.

We followed the same practice of staying in a hotel at midday. Because this was a three-day run I had to wait until the school term finished, so we started out on December 22nd. Besides being cold throughout, in the low forties, it was the shortest day of the year, so I had to cut down on my rest periods in order to finish in daylight. The pattern was again one of progressive fatigue and stiffness but bearing in mind my previous experience I slowed down a bit, walking a mile or two at the end of the day. I managed 50 miles on the first day, and we stayed in very comfortable surroundings at the Antrobus Arms in Amesbury.

The next day I had to struggle against a headwind and some switchback hills across Salisbury Plain, but I did 47 miles that day and 43 the next, which was Christmas Eve. The things I remember most about it were the radio reports of the Apollo 9 mission, in which men made the first ever orbit of the moon. I carried a little transistor radio, to stave off boredom, and I felt that I really shared in the experience of those astronauts on my own long journey. I finally arrived in Exeter after dark on Christmas Eve. I spent Christmas mainly in a seated position, partly because I was eating and drinking large amounts and partly because I had stiffened up so much that any movement of the joints was painful.

The body can react to exorbitant exercise in two ways—either it can adjust so as to be ready for the next exercise or it can stiffen up so much that no further exercise is possible for a long time. If I stiffened up badly after 150 miles, what was going to happen after 1,500? The answer to this was not really resolved until my last big run, during the half-term holiday at the end of February. I had tried to keep up a weekly mileage of 130 to 150 miles during January and February, in spite of the cold, the darkness both night and morning and the fact that the footpath was often flooded. The children at school had got used to seeing me in my running clothes, they now got used to seeing me wet through. Anyway, it paid off. I did 220 miles in five days, partly at home and partly at the hotel in Hampshire where my grandmother lived. I was now running in shorter stages than before, nothing further than 15 at a stretch, and at a rather slower pace. To my delight I found that I could run as far on the fifth day as on the first, with no more effort, and without much stiffness. I still had six weeks left but felt that I was as well prepared as I could be, for a part time runner.

During most of this time it was by no means certain that my training was ever going to be put to the test. Although several organisations had shown interest, they were not keen to put money into something with so much apparent risk of failure. After six months of writing letters and seeing people, I had firm promises of support from three sources—Pan American Airways, British Leyland Motors and Caravans International. British Leyland had agreed to lend us two cars and Caravans International a Sprite 400 caravan for the duration of the trip, in return for the publicity which we hoped they would be able to get during the course of the run. The reason for asking for the extra car was that I felt I would need to have one vehicle close to me all the time, if I was to run with the minimum amount of trouble. I would have to have the caravan there to rest in during my stops, which meant that there would not be time for the car towing the caravan to go either back or on ahead when we got into the open spaces. I judged, correctly, that there would be many times when we would need an extra person to go ahead, to arrange accommodation, rendezvous with press or TV, pick up mail or get food and drink.

Besides this there was the safety factor. With only one accompanying vehicle and one person, a single mechanical failure or bout of illness could put the whole project at risk. This led us to the problem of finding the third person, someone whom we could trust completely, and with whom we could live at close quarters for three months without driving each other crazy. Although David MacJannet could not make it, we didn't have to look far for a substitute, because my cousin Mark, who had just left school, volunteered to come. Not only was he a good driver and mechanic, but he was the ideal person as far as fitting in to the party was concerned. He lived near us, had been to the same school as me, and was Clive's godfather; the common background we shared meant that we could communicate far more easily than with someone, however enthusiastic, brought in from outside.

By the end of December, I had to make up my mind whether or not I was going to have a shot, as I had to give a term's notice to my school. I was confident that I would find the means of going, and my headmaster very kindly said that they would take me back in the following September if I took a term's unpaid leave. We kept on with our plans, made our reservations, got our injections, visas and passports in order, and I kept on writing letters. As I had hoped, two more possibilities became firm offers of assistance, I got an agreement with *The Observer* for a weekly story which I would write for them, and an agreement with Thames Television for the rights of TV film of the run. Thames sent a crew down to film 'A day in the life of a long-distance runner', which gave us a lot of amusement and raised my prestige enormously among the junior members of the school. On the strength of these agreements I borrowed enough money to equip us and cover our costs in America, and we made firm arrangements to leave Britain on April 3rd, and to start the run from Los Angeles on April 19th. It was only after doing all this that our luck really turned, when I was rung up by Commander Whitehead, of Schweppes. In Britain, Schweppes mineral waters have been part of the social scene for a long, long time, but in the United States they are still breaking new ground. It was a fortunate day for us when they decided to sponsor my record attempt. All our running expenses would be covered by them; this meant that I would have no financial worries during the trip, and that my writing and TV contracts would become profit.

One of the problems brought up was how I was going to prove that I had done it. We solved this in two ways—firstly, I resolved never to run in darkness, this meant that the press, the highway patrols or any individual could check up on my whereabouts at any time during the run. Secondly, we had a special log and witness book printed for us by our friend Trevor Wells. In this we could record the starting and finishing points, and the times, on each day's run, together with the times of passing through any towns en route and get a signature from a member of the local community to witness my progress.

The whole prospect now appeared brighter, and very exciting. Several separate trends were converging on a certain point in time—there was my training programme, and the mental preparation which we had all been making, there was the slowly growing publicity through various media, and the growing comment among our friends and relations as they realised that we really were going do to it. Finally, inexorably, there was the sequence of definite events which led to our actual departure. I had to clear up my school work, to hand over for a term, we had to settle our bills and say goodbye to our friends and relations. Term ended on April 1st. I had an Easter egg and a farewell card from my form, and a jar of foot ointment from the staff!

On Wednesday, the 2nd, we did our last bits of shopping and packed our bags, in the evening we had a very pleasant dinner with Chris Brasher and his wife Shirley. Chris, of course, is best known as the steeplechase gold medallist in the Melbourne Olympics, but he was also at that time the leading sportswriter of *The Observer*, to whom I would be sending my weekly reports.

On Thursday morning we shut the door on our little house, wondering what would happen to us before we returned three months later.

Chapter 3
Los Angeles to Blythe, CA

Thursday, April 3rd, was a very long day. Though we were not due to take off till 2 pm, we had to be at the airport by 10.30, for the benefit of the television people. I remember that we were wearing our summer-weight clothes, and though there was a bright sun there was also a strong cold wind as we stood on top of one of the airport buildings being interviewed. There was a last-minute panic when my credit card for sending cables hadn't arrived by the first post. Luckily, when I rang up the local sorting office, the postman, who was the father of one of my pupils, found it for us in the registered post.

Mark drove us to the airport—he was to fly out a week or so later; other friends and relations came out to see us off, and the last hour or so was a happy, excited bustle. Clive had not flown since he was a very small baby; dozens of times he had come to the airport to see me off on some athletic trip, and now he was going all the way to Los Angeles. We flew on Pan American, of course, since they were assisting us, and the eleven-hour flight passed much more quickly than we had expected. It helped having Clive with us, to explain it all to—he never slept once throughout the flight! It was a most impressive sight to fly over the Canadian snowfields, crossing mountains and glaciers for what seemed like hours without seeing any sign of human activity. Flying in over the California mountains, however, aroused different feelings; it was at once frightening and exciting to see mile upon mile of barren ranges and scrubland, with only the occasional strip of road, and to think that I had to get across this on foot.

We landed in Los Angeles at 4.30 pm, thanks to the nine-hour time difference, and it took another hour before we got through formalities and a few photographs, to be met by our friends Richard and Harriet Romo. Richard had spent some time in England in 1963, and had run for my club, Portsmouth AC After returning to his native Texas he had a distinguished running career, becoming the first Texan to break four minutes for the mile, and narrowly missing the US team. Both he and his wife were now teaching in Los Angeles. They looked after us very well and gave us a fixed base in what is a most confusing city. Through them we met others in the distance-running fraternity, members of the Los Angeles Striders. It was a striking contrast to the running scene in London, where there are a score of clubs in an equivalent area, to find only a single club in Los Angeles, with its members spread in an area of 50 miles radius. Even on the West Coast, it is hard for an athlete to continue training and competing after he leaves college.

This is foreign to my view of sport during school and college years. Surely the idea should be to develop interest and physical talent so that the individual enjoys a lifetime of healthy recreation, rather than push him through a highly competitive system and then abandon him just at the time when he is at his best. Still it was good to meet a few dedicated followers of the sport, and to train with such runners as Gene Comroe and Bob Deines. We had one superb marathon training run, a group of six or seven of us going up into the Santa Monica hills, with flowering trees around us and looking down on the dwellings of the rich in Bel Air, and the Pacific Ocean beyond.

I ran the marathon distance in about 2 hours 45 minutes—not a fast time by racing standards, but I felt very easy and fresh. Curiously enough, on that run I met one of the only people I knew in the enormous city, the former Hungarian coach Mihaly Igloi. In earlier years I had had some tremendous races with his record-breaking protégés, Tabori, Iharos and Roszavolgyi, and in particular I remember meeting Laszlo Tabori with Igloi at the Edinburgh Highland Games of 1960, when they were touring Europe. We had a very close race, which I eventually won by inches, my bare feet being better suited to the soft grass track than his spikes. It was a strange thing to meet his former coach, wrapped up in all these faraway European memories, in the changeless California sunshine.

Apart from a not-too-strenuous training programme, there was a good deal of work to do, but the main benefit of the two weeks we spent in Los Angeles before the start was in becoming mentally acclimatised. Noel Coward once said of America: 'there is nothing between us but the language.' He was right, it is a foreign country, and the common language only serves to conceal the enormous differences in values, priorities and basic assumptions which derive from different historical backgrounds and from the physical nature of the country. In my first article written for *The Observer* I started as follows:

> *There is one quiet place in Los Angeles, it is the Union Railroad Station. Here the air blows cool through the colonnades and your footsteps echo on the marble. Inside is like St. Peter's in Rome; outside is the world of the automobile. No amount of advice can prepare you for the experience of Los Angeles, it hits you like a blast from a furnace, the size, the noise, the fumes, the lights, the freeways and above all, the traffic surround and envelope the individual. In California, European values cease to apply, and one is left floundering, looking for a fixed point on which to anchor that precarious raft of ideas that one calls a personality. The overwhelming impression of life in Los Angeles is one of impermanence and impersonality. Nobody belongs here, everybody is from somewhere else. Nobody intends to stay in their job, everybody wants to move on and move up. On Monday it was announced that the Chief of Police is resigning in order to become a TV newscaster, but that doesn't strike anyone as odd. They figure that maybe he'll be running for Mayor in a few years' time, so he needs to get his face well known. In a place where personal communication is minimal, a man is as big as his public image, but where image-making is a major industry, what can you believe? It comes out that you can only believe in yourself. As the hippies here would say, I am 'doing my thing', and people can make what they like out of it. I may come out as a hero, or a crank, or merely as another Californian curiosity.*

On the purely mechanical side things went ahead according to plan. I had several discussions with Schweppes' publicity agents, as a result of which it was decided to postpone the starting date by two days, until Monday, April 21st, since this was likely to give us better news coverage. We attended a sports writers' luncheon, a sports newscasters' luncheon, a press conference held at the British Consulate and a party given by the Striders. We did several TV and radio interviews, and I had photographs taken of me wearing the special Schweppes running gear I would be using on the run. This consisted of shorts, t-shirts, sweaters and tracksuit trousers, all in a brilliant golden yellow, which was the colour of the Schweppes Tonic Water label. It also happened to be a good colour for the job, since it reflected the sunlight well, reducing heat, and was highly visible to traffic.

In the second week of our stay we moved out to Riverside, 50 miles east of Los Angeles, where we had been invited to stay with our friends Robert and Suzanne Seymour. They had lived near us for several years while Robert was on a tour of duty at the High Wycombe Air Force Base, and had only recently moved to California, so we had a lot to talk about, mainly village gossip! Clive enjoyed it a lot, as their little girl was just a bit older than him, and they spent most of their time splashing about in the pool. We took them to Disneyland one day, which was absolute paradise for them, and amusing for us as well.

Soon after our arrival British Leyland Motors had provided us with one of our cars—an Austin America—which, though it looked tiny beside the American cars, was ideal for us, handling in a way to which we were accustomed, and made the adjustment to American road conditions much easier. We soon got used to driving on the right, and found the huge freeway system, though awe-inspiring and even frightening at first regard, to be logical and easy to use. Mark arrived a week after us, and not long after him the second car, which had been towing the caravan across the country from Baltimore, was delivered. Mark and I went to the garage to collect it, and to his joy we found that it was a white MGB convertible. As Mark is a sports car fanatic, he claimed this as his own, and from then on, he took over responsibility for the mechanical side of things, at which he was extremely efficient.

Sue and I still had some work to do in connection with the send-off and the publicity surrounding it; in this connection we had a lot of help from the British Consulate, and from John Houlton in particular. It was arranged that we should start from the steps of City Hall, and that either Mayor Sam Yorty or one of his staff would see me off, witness my departure in the book I had brought from England for the purpose, and hand me a message to be delivered to Mayor Lindsay in New York. We went into the centre and drove over the route I would take to get out of the city. This was by no means straightforward, as all the main roads were freeways, and therefore forbidden to pedestrians. We spent another day looking over the route I would take on the second day, this too involved detours from the direct route.

A crucial day came when the Schweppes PR man, Maury Soward, was due to arrive from New York. As he was going to travel the whole way with us, we were curious to know what he was like. He proved to be middle-aged, of Canadian origin, obviously well-educated and obviously dedicated to the task of promoting our sponsor's products—at our first dinner together, he insisted on drinking only Schweppes Tonic Water. He brought with him a set of signs to go on the sides of the vehicles, and we spent a day out at Riverside sticking them on. Maury was to travel in a Volkswagen camper, so that he would be free to go on ahead of us when necessary.

The last few days were very busy, and we were glad to have the extra weekend. On the last Friday night Suzanne gave a party for us, at which the drinks were pretty strong, and everyone got very abandoned. The next morning Sue and I flew up to San Francisco for the day, everyone had told us we must see it, and as we didn't know when we'd be on the West Coast again, we felt we mustn't miss the opportunity. I was very glad we didn't, for its charm and beauty were immediately apparent; I felt that here was a city for which I could feel affection, which was not true of Los Angeles, however many friends we had there.

The last day, Sunday, was spent in loading up the cars and the caravan. We had managed to buy everything we thought we needed except snake-bite antidote. When we tried to get some of that, we were told that there had been a run on it lately and they were sold out—a comforting thought! We had sleeping bags, cooking equipment, folding table and stools for eating outside, a dozen bottles of Elliman's Athletic Rub which I had brought from England, and crates of Schweppes. We were presented at the last minute with about 50 pounds of Cadbury's milk chocolate, but delicious as it is, and useful as an energy food, we could only take a few bars with us. The thought of travelling through the desert with fifty pounds of melted milk chocolate was too awful to contemplate!

Most of my luggage was running kit and shoes. We were being provided with shoes by Adidas, the West German firm, whose track shoes I had worn in the past. They had sent me both marathon shoes and 'warm ups', which are a heavier training shoe. Both have firm micro-cellular rubber soles, foam rubber inside and soft, light leather uppers.

Equipped and rested, we drove down to City Hall in good time on the Monday morning, arriving soon after nine. There was no sign of Maury, but as we waited, more and more people arrived—representatives of Schweppes, including our friend Jack Jacks, a convivial Falstaff of a man; representatives of Cadbury's chocolate; several from British Leyland Motors; and the inevitable photographers and newsmen. A bowler hat appeared, and underneath it was our friend Dick Bank, a track and field journalist, who wanted to make us feel at home, so he said! Maury eventually turned up—his watch had stopped. This was the third minor crisis since he had arrived—the others had been losing his wallet on the first day and trying to fill his water tank without putting the plug in, and I began to wonder whether he would survive the crossing.

The final parties to arrive were the British Consul, Mr Franklin, and his wife, with John Houlton, and a representative from Mayor Yorty, who was otherwise occupied. As the next mayoral election was only a few weeks away, one couldn't blame him. We got all the pictures taken, and the witness book was duly entered to signify that I had left City Hall, Los Angeles, on foot.

I took off my sweater and tracksuit bottoms, so that I was wearing just t-shirt, shorts, shoes and socks, I carried a street map and my dark glasses. As the clock on the tower jerked to ten o'clock, I set off.

I trotted briskly round the comer of the City Hall, nipped across the road while the lights were green and was on my way eastwards, up Main Street. I passed the old Plaza, which had once been the centre of the old Spanish town, the City of Our Lady, Queen of the Angels, now drowned under a sea of concrete; I passed the Union Station and turned on to Mission Road. Soon Mark passed me, driving the MGB with the caravan behind; a TV car cruised alongside me, filming. I felt very good to be on my way, after so much planning and worrying. It was just up to me now—my willpower and my legs. In the first hour I covered over nine miles, in spite of having to wait for the occasional traffic light and stop for a TV interview.

The second hour was rather harder, as the sun got higher. The road ran northeast and then curved to the east. I ran on the south side of the road, so as to get the maximum shade from the buildings. There are very few pedestrians on the streets, so there was no problem there, but after a time I found the cumulative effect of hopping on and off the pavement to be rather tiring; as with any kind of running, economy of effort is everything, and with the pavement nine inches above the road, there is an appreciable jar each time one comes off it, and an extra push required when one steps up on to it again.

At twelve noon I stopped for a drink and a rest. Normally I would have stopped for a long break at this time but having started at ten I couldn't do this. I had come 18 miles, and had passed the San Gabriel Mission, which in the old Spanish days had been set up one day's journey from Los Angeles. After 20 minutes I set out for another six miles. The sun was right overhead, and I was finding it hard work. Possibly I had been running too fast, pushed on by the first impulse of a will that had to last me the whole 66 days. Whatever it was—the sun or the carbon monoxide of the traffic fumes—I felt very uncomfortable, but had to keep on till I reached the caravan. Sue was waiting there, having taken it over while the others went back to Riverside for the afternoon. Luckily the last of the TV people had left us, for when I got inside the caravan and sat down, I got the most violent cramp in both thigh muscles. I stood up and tried to straighten my legs, to stretch out the cramped muscles. When I sat down again, I had an overwhelming feeling of nausea, and then passed out for a few seconds.

I lay back on the bunk, with my brain racing. I had only been going three hours. Was it going to be like this all the way? Was I going to risk sunstroke by going on? Then logic took over, I had ten weeks to beat the record; I could take all the time I needed to get used to the conditions; I could walk for a week if necessary—the thing now was to treat myself for the condition I was in. Poor Sue was dreadfully worried, and I knew she was thinking the same things as I was. The cramp was obviously due to excessive salt loss, so I took two salt tablets straight away, with a pint of drink, then I sponged myself thoroughly and had a half hour rest, while Sue got lunch ready. By 3.15 I was ready to start again. We decided not to mention this crisis to anyone, it would have thrown too much doubt on my ability to finish, whereas I was sure myself that it was the start which was the hardest part, and that it would become much easier later on.

In the afternoon it was decided that Sue would go back to Riverside, and Maury would look after me, as there was no point in everybody hanging about in the sun and the dust. All went well during the first hour; I deliberately kept drinking a lot, to keep up my fluid balance, but as Maury only had Schweppes fizzy drinks I began to feel like an inflated balloon. I turned south for a mile or so, down to Pomona, and crossed underneath the eastbound freeway, so as to get myself on to the road out to Ontario. In Pomona I had to go through a subway and then turn east on Mission Boulevard. Having completed this manoeuvre, I looked for Maury with a drink, but there was no sign of him, nor did I see him again for a further 40 minutes. I went on and on down an endless road lined with motels, garages and bars, past the giant hoardings advertising Coca-Cola and beers.

Finally, I stopped for a drink of water in a filling station. Eventually Maury came along again; he said he must have missed me, he was very sorry. For the last part of the day's run Sue came out to meet me. The day's total was 46 miles, taking me to a road junction south of Ontario, at Mira Loma. There was no one about, and the sun was setting, when I climbed into the Austin and returned to the comfort of the Seymour's house in Riverside. So ended the first day.

I didn't sleep very well. The sun was still shining in my dreams, beating on my head. I was pretty stiff the next morning, in spite of showers and massage, but it eased off when I started running. Mark took me back to Mira Loma at 7 am, and I did five miles before breakfast; Sue took the trailer to a suitable spot just off the road, so that when I arrived breakfast would be ready. Unfortunately, this didn't work out. Clive and his friends had managed to put down the inside catch on the lock while playing in it the day before, and eventually we had to break in through a window. Still I enjoyed my first breakfast on the road with a good appetite.

While we were there a radio car came by for a brief interview. A little way down the road I had a charming reception from the people of Riverside—the Mayor drove down to meet me and a school band came out and played cheerful music, in the corner of a supermarket car park. The man who had organised it all, Charles Ferguson, even ran a mile down the road with me.

After all this attention I felt quite enthusiastic about the day's task, especially as it was cloudy and cooler than the day before. We said goodbye to Suzanne and her family and felt that we were cutting our last links with the familiar world and casting ourselves out into a sea of unknown experiences. The morning run led me through the orange groves, the scent of blossom everywhere, out into semi-desert country to the vast March Air Force Base, from where the huge bombers of Strategic Air Command set out to patrol a quarter of the world, from the Rockies to the coast of China. How trivial our own enterprise seemed against this glimpse of global reality.

During the second day's run I had to make a detour to the south, to avoid the freeway, which added about 14 miles to the most direct route, but I had taken this into account. It was an uneventful day and gave us a chance to settle down to what was to become our daily routine, with the vehicles going three or four miles ahead of me and waiting for me to come up for a drink or a sponge. The first part of the route was a little longer than I expected, but in the afternoon a reporter from the *Riverside Gazette* came out, and she showed me where I could save a couple of miles. The last part of the day was hard, as I had to turn north and make a climb of almost 2,000 feet in six miles to reach Beaumont, our second night's stop. However, just as darkness was approaching, and I was feeling tired, Sue came down the road to meet me, having been into Beaumont to find a resting place. A bunch of boys from San Jacinto college stopped too and jogged a little way. Thus encouraged, I reached Beaumont just as darkness fell.

That night we stayed in our first trailer park, where the owner kindly refused payment. I staggered off to the showers and Sue got supper ready. I had done 47 or 48 miles and went to bed before ten o'clock. On the morning of the third day I felt very stiff. I started before seven, and walked out of Beaumont towards Banning, six miles away. When I tried to jog, the front of my thigh muscles felt tight as hell. I walked again, then tried jogging for 50 paces. I walked again, then tried jogging for 100 paces. My stride length was about two feet, I had to lean forward and shuffle along like an old man!

We stopped just outside Banning for breakfast, and this time we were much better organised. There is nothing nicer than sitting down with a good appetite, to eat a fresh grapefruit, with bacon frying in the pan. The Highway Patrol stopped to talk to us and told me what to expect on the road ahead; I was now through that range of hills, and had a slight downgrade to Palm Springs, but there was a report of the wind getting up, and a sand storm blowing up. One of the police officers said he might fly down later and see how I was doing—he had his own plane! The headmaster of the local elementary school stopped for a chat too; he was little older than I was, but driving a new Porsche—you don't see many of those parked outside English schools, unless it's Parents' Day. The general level of prosperity in California never ceased to amaze us.

For a few miles I ran alongside the freeway, on the old road which now served as a frontage road. The country was now desert—not the traditional shifting sands one might expect, but arid reddish soil covered in low prickly shrubs, among which one could hear the lizards scuttling, and see the occasional gopher. It was warm, getting into the eighties, but up on my right, to the south, the mountains climbed up to the snow-capped peak of San Jacinto only a few miles away. I was running through a gradually widening valley and at the end of it, where the hills met the open desert, I could see the reddish haze of a dust storm. We stopped for our mid-morning break almost in the centre of it.

The wind came down the valley from the west at about 40 mph, the dust filtered in round the edge of the windows and settled on everything. When I got out to run again the wind blew me along almost faster than my stiff legs would bear, but once I got round the corner and headed in a more southerly direction towards Palm Springs things improved, the mountains sheltered me from the worst of the wind, and we were out of the dust.

By lunchtime I was feeling better, I ran into the centre of Palm Springs, and we parked in the car park of a television studio, where I was to have an interview with Don Wilson, one of America's veterans of TV, now semi-retired in Palm Springs. We were struck, as we had been before, by the extremely cavalier fashion in which television companies treat people in the States. In a similar situation in England we would at least have been given lunch, but in the States, you are just so much camera fodder, and lucky to be on TV at all.

Anyway, Clive and I were interviewed by Don Wilson, a most charming and relaxed man, and after a short rest I took the road to India, leaving Palm Springs behind me. It was hard to see why this little place should have attracted so many wealthy Americans. It had little architectural merit, though it suffered much less from billboards and advertisements than most Californian towns we saw, and though the climate is warm and dry it can also be unpleasantly hot and dusty.

With the interview, having to go out for lunch and then to the bank, I didn't perhaps rest quite as much as I should have done, and that afternoon run was tiring. The temperature got up to nearly 90°, and only a few weeks before I had been doing all my training in 40° to 50° temperatures. I was taking careful precautions to protect myself from this change of climate. Before going out in the afternoon sun I would put on sun cream, dark glasses, a silk scarf round my neck and a peaked cap to protect my head. Every three miles I would sponge myself down with cold water and drink about half a pint of cold orange juice diluted down. If I had been sweating a lot, I would take a salt tablet as well. Towards the end of the day

I would discard cap, scarf and shirt, in order to improve my suntan and become less dependent on these artificial forms of protection. It worked out very well, because after that first day I never suffered from cramp, and never from sunburn or heat exhaustion.

The end of that day was pretty hard, partly because of lack of rest at lunchtime. Maury went on ahead to find a trailer park near India, and after the mid-afternoon break, when I had already done 40 miles, he came back to tell us he had found a place about five miles up the road. Now I have come to be a very good judge of pace and distance; I managed four miles at a decent pace, in spite of feeling increasingly stiff and tired, then had to walk for a bit, expecting to have a mile left. After a mile there was no sign of a trailer park—we were in a forest of date palms in that area—so I went on, alternately jogging and walking, as it got darker and I went further, I got more and more fed up; at last, when I'd run 48 miles, Mark came to pick me up. As it was dark I couldn't have gone on safely any longer, though I was still a mile short of the night's camp. When we arrived, we pointed out to Maury that an extra mile or two may not matter much if one is in a car, but it is rather significant if you are on foot, especially if it is a tired foot.

The day hadn't ended there. Apparently, some of the Schweppes distributors wanted to take us out to dinner, so we dressed and went into India, where we had a drink and met some people, I was feeling a bit tired and irritable, and didn't take very kindly having my photograph taken again and being asked the same set of questions again. I did another radio interview, and then everybody disappeared, leaving Maury to pay for our dinner! We did however meet a very enthusiastic couple from England, Mr and Mrs Harry Boyd, who presented us with several jars of their home-made marmalade, it was delicious, and lasted us all the way to New York. After dinner we all felt better tempered, but I was rather struck by the difference in the code of manners which seemed to apply in business, as opposed to private hospitality.

It had been a tiring day and it was to get tougher. The fourth day was entirely across desert, crossing quite a high range of hills and finishing up at the aptly named Desert Center. I ran into and through India before breakfast, starting at 6 am. After breakfast I struck out for the hills and managed a good pace in spite of the steady climb. The country became browner and even more arid, the temperature rose, but I felt that I was getting more used to the task and was more cheerful than the day before.

We were being accompanied as far as the Arizona border by reporters from the *Riverside Enterprise*, as we were running through Riverside County, and that day we had Rex Nevins with us, with whom we got on very well. We stopped for lunch in blazing sun, in the Joshua Tree Memorial Park. Nothing more unlike the traditional green English park could be imagined—the wrinkled brown desert spread up to the brown hills, punctuated by the flame-like blossom of the ocotillo trees. Rex found a place to get water, so that I could sponge off the sweat, which was pouring of me. As we had driven a mile off the road, we were free for once of traffic noise, and I dozed off after lunch, only the crickets sang in that still expanse, their trilling seemed to be the noise of the sun itself, vibrating on the hot surface of the planet.

The road to Desert Center, which I took that afternoon, is very straight. I was on Route 60, an Interstate Highway, with two lanes and a wide shoulder on each side. I ran on the right of the road, on the shoulder, and every minute or so I could hear a truck coming up behind me. I braced myself as it whooshed past me at 60 mph or more and a blast of hot air bulleted me from behind. I soon got to know the names of these giants— Lee Way, Consolidated Freight, Transcontinental and Navajo—and some of the truck drivers must have passed me several times during my two months on the road. Occasionally we would pass a truck drivers' pull-in, with the great grey beasts huddled together like oblong elephants while their drivers shared a coffee and a break from the monotony of that long straight road.

On this stretch there was nothing to relieve the tedium at all, and if I could see a green road sign ahead of me, I would quicken my pace to get within reading distance of it. At tea-time we had a pleasant interlude, when we met an Indian trader who stopped to see what I was doing. He was an interesting man; he drove around buying and selling Indian jewellery, as well as making it himself. In the front of his truck, much to Clive's delight, he had a life-size wooden Indian for company. He presented me with a little pin, in the form of a road-runner, which I wore on my shirt. The road-runner bird is a familiar symbol in the West. The bird itself can be seen dashing across the road with its neck stretched out in front of it, and its long tail behind. It is a foolish bird—perhaps a good emblem for our crazy enterprise.

Towards the end of the afternoon my right thigh muscle began to stiffen up, I had to alternate jogging and walking as it became more painful, and eventually decided to call it a day when still five miles short of my goal; I had covered 47 miles that day, and saw no point in pushing on too hard when there was a risk of injury. As Mark drove me down a gentle incline leading to Desert Center, I could see a gas station, a few bungalows and a huddle of trailers, and beyond that nothing at all, as far as the brown line where desert met sky 40 miles away.

It was hard to imagine why anyone should want to live in these conditions, and yet we found quite a thriving little community. Some were involved in maintenance of the roads, telephones and water supplies, some in geological work, some lived here just out of preference for the quiet, and some just seemed to have drifted here and failed to move on. There was none of the ingrowing feeling that one sometimes finds in isolated communities, like some of the out-of-the-way villages in my native Devon, and I suppose the answer is communication. Everyone there could easily be in India or Palm Springs in an hour's drive and even if they stayed put, they were as much in touch with the life of the nation through television as anyone in an apartment in New York. They had one characteristic of small communities, though: they were very friendly to strangers. We met a charming family of South Africans, who were living there for a while in the course of a journey round the world, when we left, we were presented with some bacon and eggs, and also with three pairs of bed socks! They were coloured in red, green, blue and white, with white bobbles on, and white woolly laces that tied round the ankle, giving them the appearance of boxing boots. We tried them on, and the effect was so ludicrous that Sue was reduced to helpless giggles, but the time came when we were very glad of them—and it was a very kind thought too.

After four days I had covered 187 miles, but the fifth day brought the average down a bit. I was taken five miles back down the road, and covered that stretch in about an hour, before breakfast. We got a bit delayed trying to put through a call to Thames Television, but I wasn't worried, as I had all day. When. I started out again, though, it was apparent that I would need it all, for my right thigh soon stiffened up so much that all I could do was walk with a limp. I limped along from 8.30 till 10.30, from 11 till 1 pm, and then took a long siesta out of the sun. I managed a further three hours walking, with one break, before the swift approach of night soon after seven o'clock. The seven hours of walking had only taken me 25 miles, leaving me 20 miles short of Blythe, my scheduled resting place, and my day's total was a miserable 30 miles.

Strange to say, I did not at the time feel very depressed about this slow progress. For one thing, walking is much less energetic than running, so I did not heat up so much, I wore my full Lawrence of Arabia garb—peaked cap, scarf and sunglasses—without discomfort. For another thing I was due that evening to send off my first on-the-road despatch to *The Observer*, and I therefore had plenty of time to choose my words, memorise phrases and try out different beginnings and endings in my head.

I made a start, too, on what was to become a regular time-wasting device—that of calculating my daily average, and how long it would take me to get to New York, at different daily mileages. The end of this day gave me 217 miles in five days—an average of 43—which was just what I had set myself. On the other hand, I was still 20 miles behind my published schedule. I decided to myself that as the five days were not up till ten o'clock on the following day, Saturday, I would try to reach Blythe by that time if it were reasonably possible.

We had a certain amount of diversion in the afternoon. Down the centre of the divided highway was a broad median, mostly rather sandy. We had parked the trailer there at lunchtime, and Mark had had a bit of trouble getting it out. Just as he had got it on to the shoulder, we saw Maury's camper approaching from the east—he had gone into Blythe to make phone calls. We saw him zoom past us, then notice us; what followed was utterly predictable, he went a couple of hundred yards further on looking for a suitable turning place, then swung across the median. He went too slowly and sank in, then he revved madly and got truly embedded, eventually we could see the Volkswagen immobile, up to its axles in sand. Mark went down to help, then a lorry driver stopped; together the three of them cleared away the loose sand, poured on water to give a firmer surface, and got boards under the wheels. Then they couldn't find the keys. It was nearly 90° and I don't think the truck driver appreciated the humour of the situation. The keys turned up 20 minutes later—in the door—but Mark had left by that time, so we shall never know what the truck driver said to Maury about it.

Things looked up as soon as we drove into Blythe, because the proprietor of the Blue Line Motel gave us free parking space, and a very warm welcome. I had a good shower and a massage, and we went along to a café, where we had fish and chips, ice cream and coffee. I slept soundly that night, and the next morning we started back to the finish of the previous day's run before six o'clock. I took a sandwich, a carton of milk and some fresh fruit, which I ate while Mark drove.

At 6.20 I was on the move again, at first walking and jogging alternately, then jogging most of the time. On the way out I had noted the distance of various landmarks from the town—it took me nearly an hour to get the first five miles behind me, then an hour for the next six miles, leaving only nine to go. By that time I was in sight of the outskirts of the town, and had something to run for, it was heating up, and I was getting thirsty, but I had arranged for Mark to come out to meet me with a second breakfast, and by the time the welcome silhouette of the MGB appeared on the road I was only four miles out of town. I took the last four miles pretty easily, and just after 10 am I reached our motel in Blythe. That 20 miles was the longest continuous stretch of the trip so far, but I had conquered my first major obstacle, the California desert.

Chapter 4
Blythe to Phoenix, AZ

As will become increasingly revealed during the course of the narrative, state of mind and physical condition are inextricably interwoven and interdependent. During the night I had been worrying about my stiffness and how long it would take me to get to Blythe. Once I had that 20 miles behind me, even though I was still behind schedule, my whole approach became much more optimistic. After a shower at the motel and pausing for a while to say goodbye to the people who had been so kind to us there, I set out to walk a further four miles before lunch. This took me out of Blythe and in fact out of California. The Colorado River here forms the border between California and Arizona and is spanned by a wide bridge. There is something about crossing rivers which is very meaningful to the traveller—another river behind one, like another mountain range, gives the impression, false in this case, of having surmounted another barrier. Here the wind was blowing very strongly down due river, blowing sand from the bank, fluttering my scarf and nearly taking my cap off, but this added to the excitement I felt at having at last reached another state.

We had our lunch in the no-man's land adjoining the border inspection stations. In Arizona they appear to place a lot of importance on the inspection of incoming food materials, and the huge container trucks were forced to line up for inspection before going on—probably a welcome break for the drivers.

After our lunch and a rest, I set out full of enthusiasm, my target for the night being the little town of Quartzsite, 23 miles away. As soon as I jogged up the gradient away from the river the scenery started to change, within a few hundred yards of the border I saw my first giant cactus, that characteristic desert sight, a visual cliché, beloved of cartoons. The road climbed gradually upwards and the scenery became more spectacular. The mountains of Arizona feature a lot in Western films, and many of the silhouettes appearing on the skyline seemed familiar, doubtless seen many times in those old TV Westerns at home. There were the flat-topped mesas and the jagged rocky outcrops, round which I expected to see the villains galloping down on the unsuspecting stage coach. The atmosphere of theatricality was heightened by the quality of the light, which made these distant features appear more like two-dimensional stage sets than actual rock you could touch.

As the afternoon went on these scenes came closer to me and then passed out of my line of vision, to be replaced by others of equal splendour. At one point on the slow climb I saw a strange sight—another pedestrian, the first I had seen since leaving Los Angeles. It was a man in a check shirt, walking on the left side of the road, in other words in the wrong lane for eastbound traffic. He was whittling a stick with a knife and walking very slowly. After bidding him good afternoon I enquired where he was going and found that like me, he was going to Quartzsite. He wasn't a very articulate character, but his story seemed to be that he had had to take some woman—possibly his wife—somewhere in the car, and then he'd had to leave it. 'I got hold of the dirty end of the stick there,' he kept saying. He didn't appear to be in any hurry to get back to Quartzsite, which at his pace would take him about eight hours, I calculated, if he was hitchhiking he would be on the other side of the road. I concluded that he was either very stupid or that he was lying for some reason, it is possible that he was doing some prospecting for gems or gold but wasn't going to let on. There must still be old mines around, or new ones, with a fortune for somebody.

I started jogging again, and soon was high above him on the bending road. It was not a steep climb, and the air was cooler than it had been on the flat plain; ahead of me the sky was blue over the brown hills. Eventually, at about tea-time, I came to a point where there were no more hills above me. For the last ten miles of the day's run I could see Quartzsite in front of me. In the clear air it seemed only a couple of miles away, but with my legs tiring it took me an hour-and-a-half to get there, a boring hour-and-a-half too. I finally arrived at a point just opposite the town at 6.15. The interstate highway went straight past Quartzsite only acknowledging its presence by a couple of the standardised freeway bridges, but we turned off and went to a trailer park, thereby learning far more than the normal traveller who would drive on to Phoenix.

Quartzsite is the epitome of man's ability to survive in inhospitable places. It is a community of 100 or so people, with its gas station, store and souvenir shop, surrounded by miles of emptiness. There is nothing that can be grown there, and few people stop there; there is nothing but rocks and cacti. In these conditions the people who live there put up signs saying 'Rocks for Sale' and cultivate cactus gardens. There was a sizeable trailer park which had in fact just been expanded, presumably anticipating some kind of boom—it's an optimistic country.

Along the highway to east and west of Quartzsite are the relics of old pioneer settlements of nearly 100 years ago—areas cleared of scrub and surrounded by rusty wire and containing the remains of corrugated iron shacks. Anything of any value has been collected up and may be seen at the roadside store-cum-gas station which is the only living remnant. Here one can see old boots, like the one Charlie Chaplin had for supper in *The Gold Rush* and the old kitchen chairs, shown as 'antiques'. At least Quartzsite had a trailer park with showers, and after a shower and a good meal I felt quite good. Sue cooked us veal cutlets followed by strawberries; Maury contributed a frozen fruit pie, but, as we hadn't got an oven to cook it in, it wasn't a great success.

The next morning was mercilessly clear. By nine o'clock it was already hot, and it was 37 miles to the next village, Salome. It was one of those days when each mile seems like a mile-and-a-half. I had to have a sponge down and a drink every three miles, and even that distance seemed a long way. During this day and the two succeeding days, as we approached Phoenix, the run became a personal battle, with the sun as my enemy. After a drink stop, I tried to run as far as possible without looking at my watch— usually about ten minutes. Then I would stare at my feet and try to think of something else, till five minutes had passed, by which time the car should only be a mile ahead of me, a shimmering spot in the heat. I would stare at my feet again and count to 100 at two paces to the count, then glance up to see if the car had got any closer. When things got bad, I would think of green and peaceful England, or of being down by the shore in the little Devon village I come from, sailing on the river or fishing in the rock pools.

Eventually I would arrive, to receive a lovely cold sponge and a drink from Sue, who would be patiently waiting, though getting hotter and hotter herself. In this weather, with the noonday heat well over 90°, I took a three-hour siesta. The caravan stayed surprisingly cool, and I was able to doze off into forgetfulness. I got my tape recorder out and played again and again the tape of music by Antônio Carlos Jobim, which rolled through my mind like soothing waves. When three o'clock came, and it was time to get back on the road I could resume battle, knowing that within an hour the intensity of the heat would weaken. It was always easier towards the end of the day, even though I was more tired, because each mile added brought the day's total to a better score.

The evening out of Quartzsite brought us to Salome, where I took a short cut. Study of the atlas back in England had shown a dirt road leading directly towards Phoenix, through a place called Tonopah. Sure enough, when we came to Salome there was a turn off to the south. We found a trailer park here, but it was a little early to stop for the night, so after some refreshment I set off again. The day was cooling to a beautiful evening, Sue jogged with me for two miles, and then went back to get supper, while Mark accompanied me. It was a quiet little road whose tarmac surface soon gave way to dust. The desert either side of it was covered in yellow flowering scrub, while on the hills the cacti rose up in erect columns, like a vast silent audience, somewhere up there we could hear the yelping of coyotes.

On the road behind us we heard a vehicle approaching us, and we were overtaken by a big old jeep loaded with six teenage girls. first, they wanted to know why we were running, and of course the answer produced a lot of laughter and disbelief, then some of them thought they'd get out and run with us. Two of them managed about a mile before they got back into the wagon. I said I'd try and mention them on TV when I got to Phoenix, which pleased them a lot. I was sorry to see them go, because they took my mind off the fatigue which gradually enveloped me at the end of a day's run, and I'm sure Mark was sorry to see them go too.

That day I managed 44 miles, and the next day the same. As I had originally allowed three days on the schedule for crossing this bit of desert, I was able to reach the outskirts of Phoenix exactly on schedule, on the afternoon of the 29th. All through the two days after leaving Salome we were on dirt road. We rarely saw another car, and the scene must have changed very little since the wandering Apache dominated this area 100 years ago. On my left the Big Horn mountain looked over the desert, on the road a pair of kites peeked at the carcass of a rabbit, they flapped lazily upwards as I approached, and I could hear the lizards and the gophers scuttling away between the tufts of coarse grass. As I padded through the dust, I might have been one of those Apache, and the distant cloud which surrounded our trailer might just as well have concealed a wagon train.

A few miles further on, though, there was no doubt about which century we were in. Another new highway was being pushed through towards Phoenix, and men with steel helmets and giant yellow machines were steadily reshaping the countryside to their own pattern.

The end of that day's run was supposed to be at Tonopah. A man in Salome had told us that it was a hot springs resort, but it turned out that his information was 20 years out of date. The hot springs were still there, as I found when I tried to cool myself off in some water gushing from a roadside trough, but it was no resort—there was one store, a post office which kept the name on the map, and a number of concrete foundations, already overgrown with scrub. We didn't have time to speculate on what had happened to kill the resort industry; we had to decide what to do. Tonopah had nothing to offer, and Phoenix was 40 miles away. I had a rest and some tea, while Sue went on ahead to see what she could find. I got back on to the road for the last few miles of the day, with Mark carefully steering the caravan through the dust and the potholes behind me.

We had not gone far when we met Maury, who had left us the day before to go to Phoenix. He told us that it was 35 miles to the nearest motel, which wasn't very encouraging, but I had no choice but to keep running until I had completed my quota of 43 miles. Marking the spot at which I finished, we set off towards Phoenix. We had been unable to get petrol in Tonopah, and the gauge was very low; I reckoned we had 20 miles to go before we hit the paved road but hoped we might see signs of habitation before then. Mile after mile there was nothing but scrub and cactus, then we came to three green-painted domed buildings, which apparently formed the Church of the Sun, Health and Meditation. A few miles further on another dirt track intersected ours, it was signposted 399th Avenue. This was a supreme example of American optimism, as it was just over 20 miles west of 195th Avenue—someone had obviously worked it out, at ten blocks to the mile. It looked pretty incongruous, the sign on the dirt road, but I suppose that in another 100 years it'll be just another suburban street.

As our petrol gauge showed plumb empty by now, we just coasted along, until at last we came to a couple of farmhouses, then the paved road, and at last a gas station. At that time of the day I just didn't fancy walking any distance for petrol! According to Maury's reckoning we still had 15 miles to go, but, as we pulled away from the gas station, there was a trailer park, with our trailer in it. Maury had managed to miss it on the way out of Phoenix, but Sue spotted it, and I blessed her for it. Within 15 minutes I had had a shower and a change of clothes, a cold beer inside me and was sitting down to supper, feeling a lot more cheerful than I had before.

Of all the trailer parks that we stayed in, this one made the deepest impression—it was certainly the scruffiest. The trailers were parked on what had been grass but was now mostly bare earth. Most of them had been there a long time and had sort of settled down, accumulating boxes, bottles and bits of furniture around their bases. There were dogs about, unusual in trailer parks, and a barefoot child was playing in the dirt. The people were elderly and looked as if they had stepped from a Steinbeck novel, there were a couple of fat old men in braces who moved seldom and then very slowly. There was a large grey-haired woman who spoke to Clive as he went by: 'Where ya goin', son?' she said. Clive replied, in his high-pitched English accent: I'm going to the lavatory.' 'The Laver Tree,' she said. 'What's the Laver Tree?' However, in spite of the dirt and the appalling smell in the Laver Tree, the owner was very kind and helpful; in fact, when we left, he returned the dollar we had paid him, saying 'I don't think it's worth a dollar, really.' I wondered about the economics of a place like that—his tenants didn't look as if they could afford much rent; on the other hand he had a nice clean grocery store and having a captive bunch of customers must be fairly profitable.

I had plenty of time for reflection the following morning. Mark drove me back along that 20 miles of dirt road, which I could well have done without, and then went back to the camp. For once I made an error of judgement which might have proved very uncomfortable. I asked for someone to bring me a drink in one-and-a-half to two hours, which would normally have been all right; however, it got hot early that day, and running on the dirt road meant that there was a lot of dust in the air. I started to get very thirsty, and I knew that there was no house for a long way, but my luck held. I went off the road a few yards to investigate a little hut, thinking it might have a tap, and as I was returning to the road a car came past from the construction site, we had passed the day before. They stopped to ask if I wanted anything, and, as all desert travellers should, they had a gallon of drinking water on them. Refreshed by this, I kept up a steady jog until Sue came out at the appointed time. There is a very narrow dividing line in the desert between normal life and real trouble and one can see how easy it would be to cross it, when even one hour without a drink can be unpleasant.

Once I got back to the trailer park it was easy, but the last few miles on the loose surface left their mark, in bringing about a bit of stiffness in the left thigh, which was to have serious results later. My schedule only required me to reach Goodyear that afternoon, a mere ten miles further on, so in view of the 90° heat I walked most of the way, listening to music on my pocket radio. I was back on my schedule, I had covered 400 miles of the toughest going I was likely to meet, and after a week in the desert we were booked in at a Phoenix motel for the night. During that afternoon stroll I savoured for the first time a solid sense of achievement, a consciousness of the vast tract of land that I had covered on my own feet, and of the changing nature of the country ahead of me.

Walking and jogging, I reached the road junction just North of Goodyear about four o'clock, having covered 30 miles that day. I still had 18 miles to cover to the centre of Phoenix, but at this stage of the journey I was satisfied to keep to my schedule. I felt at the time that it would probably take me two or three weeks to become adjusted to this continuous exertion, and that provided I could keep abreast of my schedule during that time I would have ample opportunity to improve upon it during the later stages. In any case it was extremely pleasant to be able to knock off at four o'clock.

In view of the publicity attaching to our arrival in a place the size of Phoenix, we were staying at Schweppes' expense in a comfortable motel—the Lazy Daze—which naturally had a pool. Mark collected a batch of letters from the Post Office, Clive had a swim, and I washed the desert dust off myself. In the evening we all dined out, with Maury, at the Neptune's Table restaurant. This was another American anomaly—a seafood restaurant hundreds of miles from the nearest salt water. They had the red lampshades, the menus two feet square and the elaborate menu phraseology, but there was one thing lacking—the real taste of fresh caught fish. If you've lived inland all your life you might think that the taste of prawn is the taste of the frozen king-size prawns in the restaurants, but it's not. I thought of the prawns I catch in Devon in the summer—dark grey-brown whiskery creatures that leap from your hand when you pick them out of the net. Pop them into boiling salt water, slide off the head and tail coverings and eat them on a slice of brown bread and butter. *That* is the taste of prawn, and every restaurateur should be forced to experience it.

The following day provided more diversions; looking back on it, it seems as long as any day in my life, because it occasioned so many different states of mind. Between 7 and 8 o'clock I ran seven miles from my stopping place, then came back for breakfast. Soon after nine I started the main run of the morning, 11 miles into the city centre. A couple of TV crews came out to film me—my stride lengthened, and my style improved. It's remarkable what a bit of attention does for the ego! One crew was particularly elegant—the newscasters appear to form a new form of aristocracy in this TV-conscious land—and drove a new white Corvette Stingray. When we reached the centre of town, we had the newspaper and radio men out to meet us as well, so we stopped for about 20 minutes to give everyone a go. Having sponged myself down once to get the sweat off me I then had to do it again for the TV people and a third time for the press photographer; I then took a drink three times and spoke to Sue three times. When I eventually got going again, I was accompanied by a young man with a tape recorder; he jogged over half a mile with me, asking questions, which I thought wasn't bad. He obviously thought it wasn't bad either, as we heard later that he played the tape 14 times on the radio in the following 24 hours!

I had lost a bit of time doing all this, so cut down a lot on my usual morning break. For one thing, we didn't have the caravan that day. The MGB had to go into the garage for the day to have a hole in the exhaust pipe repaired, which it had picked up during the rough journey from Salome; Sue was therefore driving Maury's camper for the day. As the morning went on it got very hot. The extra traffic hazards of a city—the exhaust fumes and the stepping on and off pavements—combined with the lack of rest to make me more than usually uncomfortable. Phoenix covers a large area and is growing very fast; going out on Route 60 there are literally miles of garages, motels and mobile home parks. I shall have more to say of the latter, but we were told that there were more parks in Phoenix than anywhere else in the United States and I can believe it. The warm climate and low rainfall make it a desirable spot for people in colder parts of the States, and a mobile home is the ideal answer if you want a second home in the sun. For my part I found that there was rather too much sun—over 90° at mid-day, and I was very glad when lunch-break came.

I had at long last got out of Phoenix, but the built-up area continued without a break into Tempe, which is the home of the University of Arizona. We bought a pizza for lunch—it was only Sue, Clive and I, as Mark and Maury were collecting the MGB—and we parked in the University car park to eat it and to rest. The campus contains some beautiful buildings, so Sue decided to have a stroll round, but she didn't find the usual cloistered calm: 'I walked through a quadrangle, and all these youngsters were strolling about with books under their arms, and I thought: "this is the life." Then I came out opposite a large building with big plate-glass doors. Outside it there were about 200 people, a lot of them wearing longer hair and more way-out clothes than the other students I'd seen. Standing just inside the plate-glass doors were two security guards, and it struck me that they were wearing guns; just as I was thinking "what do they need guns for, in a university?" they pushed open the glass doors and ran straight towards me. I thought: "Oh My God, I haven't done anything," and they ran straight past me and arrested a boy just behind me. They hustled him back inside the doors and the crowd started getting very upset. "They got Buzz! You all right there, Buzz? What's he done? You let him outta there!" They surged forward. Somebody broke the plate-glass doors, and this seemed to shake them a bit. They moved back and sat down and then they started singing. I thought it was time I was getting back.'

We never discovered just what the excitement was about, but we did read that 14 suspected drug pushers had been arrested at the University over the previous few days, so I suppose that was it. The only student who Sue spoke to about it said that very few of the rioters were genuine students, and that many of them had come in from elsewhere. The vast majority of the student body, he said, just wanted to get on with their degrees. This tied in with the attitude towards learning that we found across the country and agrees with the line taken by the educational establishment, but we can't claim to have taken a representative sample. As with all our days, we had to move on without hearing the full story.

The afternoon took me through Mesa, another sprawl of hot concrete along the highway. The heat coming off the pavement was worse than anything I had met in the desert. I kept sponging myself and took drinks and salt tablets till my stomach felt bloated—it couldn't absorb moisture fast enough to keep up with my sweat rate. All this time, and I was running through built-up areas from 9 am till 4 pm, I was passing roadside motels with their private pools, bars with their shaded windows, and sign after sign saying, 'Ice Cold Beer', 'Frosted Pepsi', 'Ice Cream Sundaes'. It was mental torture.

Towards the end of the day I started getting stiffness in my left thigh muscle, but I felt better mentally as the heat went out of the sun. Mark had caught up with us, and when he had left the trailer in a park up at Apache Junction, he came back to run with me. Another diversion was provided by two men from the *Mesa Tribune*, who kept popping up to take pictures, and a Swedish reporter who had flown out from Los Angeles. It was nice to meet another European, especially as Sue and I have some happy memories of holidays in Sweden. He formed a temporary bridge to a world that I could hardly believe existed, bound up as I was in this continual physical struggle.

The day ended with my walking at less than 4 mph, my leg was so stiff. Eventually Sue came and collected me three miles short of my destination, but all the same I had covered 46 miles. That night's trailer park was a distinct contrast to the last one. It was beautifully clean, with electric light and hot showers. There was quite a little crowd when I arrived—I'm afraid I disappointed them by not arriving on foot, but they made us feel very welcome. After the hard, hot, day, it was a glorious sensation just to sit down and drink cold beer, answering a few questions, then having another drink. Although I did not realise it at the time, that day marked the end of my battle against the sun, and the beginning of a new battle, against the infirmities of my own body.

Chapter 5
Phoenix to Redhill, NM

I had been running for ten days now, and had 440 miles behind me, most of it desert. I believed that the worst was behind me, whereas it was just beginning—it's a good thing we don't have foreknowledge. On the morning of May 1st my left thigh was very stiff, and there was no question of running on it. I started walking early, about 7 am, and did five miles while Sue took the trailer on ahead and prepared breakfast. I ate breakfast in the morning sun, with a good appetite, and went on walking.

When you've been running all day, walking is really very pleasant, and of course much cooler. I was gradually gaining height, the Superstition Mountains formed a barrier to the east, so the road bent away to the south for 17 miles, down to Florence Junction. Already we were high enough to escape some of the heat. I had my little radio with me, and heard the newscaster saying: 'temperatures today in the Valley of the Sun in the eighties; high today: low nineties,' but luckily we escaped that. I got in 20 miles in five hours of walking before lunch, when we had another little diversion.

Our arrival in Phoenix had apparently stirred up a bit of interest, I suppose that it became more apparent that the Transcontinental Run was a serious attempt and not just a publicity gimmick. Anyway, we were visited by a photographer who had flown out from Los Angeles, and during the lunch hour I talked on the phone at Florence Junction to their man in New York. We went back to our lunch stop, which was a shaded spot on the grass in the centre strip of the divided highway. In course of time I moved off, and Sue drove the Austin out—into the left side of the highway! Mark shouted. She immediately realised what she was doing, put the car into reverse and backed quickly, into a bollard! There was no damage done, but we wondered what the photographer thought as he sat in his car watching the performance. Anyway, it was the only lapse in thousands of miles of driving.

The afternoon passed without further incident, and my walking pace improved. Sue joined me for the last few miles, which were mostly downhill to the little mining town of Superior. It was a beautiful evening, with the hills turning red-gold in the setting sun, and the road winding down beneath us. We reached our destination just before sundown, having covered 36 miles in nine hours of walking. Superior has a history and character of its own, even though it is less than 90 years old. The life of the town centres round a great copper mine, a mile deep, that employs hundreds of miners, many of them Native Americans or Mexicans. When darkness came, we could see the molten waste glowing on the enormous slag-heap, making a round red blob, like the red eye of a monster looking out over the town. We had a long talk with the people who came from the local paper to talk to us, and one of them gave me a sample of rock from the mine. In just a few minutes we learned more of what life was like for them than we had from all the more sophisticated people we met in Phoenix.

In daylight the surroundings of Superior are even more spectacular than at night. On one side is a rocky bluff from which, 100 years ago, the Apache chief Geronimo and many of his tribe threw themselves, rather than face capture. On the northern side is a high wall of rock pierced by a narrow river gorge. The road winds up this, goes through a tunnel and climbs a total of about 2,000 feet before reaching the crest of the ridge. I tackled this before breakfast, and made good time, managing to jog most of the way up. It was on the way down that the troubles started.

During the morning my thigh muscle stiffened up again, forcing me to run with a limp. On the downhill grades I could not use this muscle for 'braking' as I would normally, so had to come down very heavily on my right foot. The scenery was very fine—ridge after ridge of brown rock, divided by wooded valleys, each with a steep river gorge in the middle, but my mind was having to concentrate entirely on my striding. On the left stride I braced the thigh muscle—*Ooh!* On the right stride I jarred my ankle—*Ouch!* I proceeded on this *Ooh!/Ouch!* basis down to the next large valley, which contained another mining town, Miami.

The road on the valley bottom being flat, I was able to jog slowly without too much pain. During the mid-morning break I talked to a couple of Native Americans who had stopped to wish me luck. They worked at the mine, had a car; they were confident, hard-working men. Not all fared so well—we saw many other Native Americans living in hopeless poverty in shacks along the road.

The twin towns of Miami and Globe share a radio station, which had clearly put out a bulletin just before I arrived, because there were a lot of people out on the street to give me a clap. The Deputy Mayor, a lady, got out of her car and ran across the road to bid me welcome, which was a nice gesture, all the more so as she was not naturally built for running. A bit further down the street I came to the local school, lying right under the great slag heap of the mine.

It wasn't much of a place—tin huts and a dusty wired-in playground— but the kids were full of enthusiasm. They came running alongside the wire to wish me luck and to shake my hand. The children were mostly Mexicans and Native Americans, and they touched me very deeply. Maybe fatigue and pain made me weaker, more easily moved, but tears came to my eyes when I left them, standing there in the dust under the slag-heap. What would happen to that enthusiasm for life? Did they stand as much chance of happiness as the kids in my form in Berkshire who were about the same age?

A few miles on I came to the Copper Hills Motel, which housed the radio station. As they wanted me to stop for an interview there, we decided to take an early lunch-break. The interview went on tape very smoothly. My interviewer was a man called Shoecraft, who had lost both his legs close to the hip. In spite of this he managed a full-time job, and, probably because of this, he had an exceptionally balanced outlook on life; one could see that he had thought about things and found his own answers.

Afterwards we all had a swim in the motel pool, which was glorious. Mark went into town to look at a gem shop. His brother is a collector, and Mark started looking at gems for him, but soon got interested in his own right. We had been told that Arizona and New Mexico were the best states for this, so were on the look-out. There wasn't much there except rather touristy copperware, and at 2.30 we were all on the road again.

After a couple of miles my right ankle started hurting again. I got into Globe, and ran through the main street, then walked a bit. A little further on I came to the high school, and there were hundreds of boys and girls beside the road, at the windows and on a bridge, which crossed the road. It was uphill, but when I saw them all I had to start running again, and they raised a cheer that brought a lump in my throat. It did nothing for the pain in my ankle, though, which became sharper and sharper. I stopped for tea at four, having done only 31 miles, and after tea I put on my leather shoes and walked, hoping that the raised heel would give more support, but it didn't help much. The others went on ahead to find a camp site, and as soon as they came back, I quit.

That day was only 35 miles, but I could feel that I was likely to run myself into serious trouble. The pain was due to inflammation of the tendons in the lower part of the right shin, a complaint familiar to road runners, who call it 'shin splint'. If you go on running on shin splints it is likely to lead to a stress fracture of the tibia—the shin bone itself. The only cure as a rule is complete rest, and it may take two or three weeks to clear up. At any rate I had a night to think about it. Sue had found a camp at a Federal Parks site called Jones Water. It was a couple of miles past what had been a silver mine village 80 years ago; now it was just a few scratchings in the hills, with the trees growing back over them. The camp site was lovely, in a little wooded valley beside a spring of pure water, there were stone tables and discreetly placed dustbins and lavatories; among the trees there were places to park a trailer and light a fire.

Clive was thrilled to be really out in the wilds, with a real camp fire, and for all of us it was soothing to be away from towns. There was only one other couple there, a man called Frank and his wife. They were taking several months to travel across the country from the Mexican border, staying in camps like this as long as they felt. They had all the right stuff for camping, and they seemed to live to a slower rhythm, speaking little and reading a lot. They whittled sticks and carved spoons, which so interested Mark that he bought a knife for carving at the next town.

We had a peaceful evening at Jones Water, but the next morning the problem was still there. I started on the road soon after eight—as it was much cooler in the hills there was no need to start very early—and it took me two hours to cover the seven miles back to Jones Water. My shin splints were pretty painful and going on would only aggravate the situation. The only hope lay in getting some strong boots, which would give more support to both foot and ankle, so Sue and I drove back into Globe, where I found just what I wanted; I felt a bit of a fraud going back to the town where I had been applauded only the day before as the great athlete, and hobbling round like a cripple.

I walked for an hour before lunch, and the boots did seem to be helping.

After lunch I managed to cover nine miles in two-and-a-half hours, with my ankle gradually becoming more painful. The only way I could keep moving was by taking all the weight on my left leg, and taking a short stride with my right, flexing the ankle as little as possible. There was one small consolation in that I had sent off my piece to *The Observer* on Friday afternoon, up to which point I was still on my schedule, so my family at home wouldn't be worrying about me.

As far as the record went, I was 40 miles up on the schedule which would beat Shepherd's time when my serious injury problem started. That day I finally quit after having done 19 miles, thereby losing over 20 miles. As I limped along the road, I kept doing sums in my head to calculate how long it would take me, if the injury lasted a week—this was really the only way to prevent despair from creeping in. The longer I went on walking, the greater would be the mileage necessary in the later stages of the run, but I was sure that I would be able to get up to 50 miles a day or more towards the end. If I had to walk for a week, at 30 miles a day, then a week of running 50 miles a day would bring me back to an average of 40—sufficient to beat the record, if not to achieve my 66-day target.

Apart from these calculations, I tried taking a book with me, as I was walking so slowly. It was Gunter Grass's *The Tin Drum*, which I found to provide a striking contrast to the uncomplicated mental world in which I lived for most of the day. I could manage to read a page of this and still keep myself on the edge of the road. Later in the day my ankle became so painful that I needed to concentrate on walking as efficiently as possible. When I decided I could not go on without risking more trouble I just sat down on the side of the road with my book. The temperature up in the hills was delightful, in the mid-sixties, with a bright sun and a fresh breeze which carried huge white clouds like galleons sailing over the peaks. I felt in very good health, just annoyed at the injury which was limiting me to this ridiculously slow pace. Nothing would have been more pleasant than to run along this winding, road between the pinewoods.

Ahead of me lay a place we had heard a lot about as we approached the mountains—the Salt River Canyon. 'Wait till you hit them hills', they had said, 'that Salt River Canyon is really something.' Some people had asked me how I was going to cross the canyon, to which I replied: 'down one side and up the other!' As there was a road marked through it I felt sure that it wouldn't be that bad; it is common human nature to make things sound worse than they are, and I knew that if the highway went through it, then it wouldn't be any problem to a man on foot, though it might slow me down a little climbing up it.

We made our camp that night actually in the canyon. We found a parking place close to the river, and as it was still quite early there was time to scramble down to the river bed and sunbathe on the rocks. We paddled in the shallow stream and tasted the brown brackish water from which the river gets its name.

I have never seen the Grand Canyon, but though it is larger I cannot believe that it is any more beautiful than the Salt River Canyon. As one comes over the hill a great panorama is revealed, the earth cleft into sections by the river and its tributaries, each section revealing its strata, like a gigantic layer-cake. The forces of wind and rain have played on these surfaces, hollowing and sculpturing, leaving patches of soil where trees grow out, little touches which provide the scale, and make the immensity of this great work of nature still more impressive. Down at the bottom one can see a bridge, and two little dolls' houses which turn out to comprise the store and filling station.

The nearest town, Globe, is over 30 miles away, the point marked on our map as Seneca turned out to consist of three or four ramshackle huts inhabited by Native Americans with large families as we were in the Apache Reservation. The next town to the North was Show Low, over 40 miles away. It was fortunate in a way that I happened to be injured in that part of the country, as it gave us some time to appreciate the most spectacular scenery we were to encounter in the whole of our way across. In fact, the Salt River Canyon was the only place in the United States apart from Los Angeles and New York where we stayed for more than one night.

My worry had eased a little bit; I was determined to be patient and go easily till my ankle improved. I therefore had a bit of a lie-in on the morning of Sunday, May 4th, before being driven back to my starting-point. Clive was thoroughly enjoying the camping out, building fires and washing in the river, Mark had employed himself usefully by making me a strong walking stick. As I would be walking, I dressed myself in khaki slacks, blue shirt and spotted cravat—Sue said I looked like the squire going out for a walk round the estate-and I set out to enjoy the ten-mile stroll down the canyon to our camp. I found that Mark's stick helped a lot in taking the weight off my bad ankle, and I was able to limp along quite briskly, taking only two-and-a-half hours and arriving in plenty of time for lunch.

In the afternoon Mark came with me for a couple of miles as I started to walk up the further side of the canyon, and then Sue took over for a bit of exercise. We went on for a couple of miles, climbing steadily, but not so steeply as to be uncomfortable. As we rose higher, we could see further along the canyon, there were dark clouds moving up on us. The far side of the canyon disappeared into cloud and it began to rain. There was nothing we could do about it, so we just went on walking. All of a sudden, the rain changed to a violent storm, hammering down on us out of a black cloud. We dashed for cover, but there was none, only some prickly bushes into which we tried to wriggle. The rocks offered no protection, as the rain was coming down vertically. It changed to hail, rattling on the shiny black road, then suddenly it was gone again. It was still raining, but with normal intensity, so like drowned rats we walked on again. We had only gone 100 yards when Mark roared up, we scrambled in, and headed back to camp. He had realised how bad it was getting when it passed over him, for which we were very grateful. After only ten minutes of storm the water was pouring down the sides of the canyon in rivulets, carrying stones out on to the road.

I had only done 15 miles that day but decided to do no more; it kept on raining for most of the evening, and during the night it really poured. I woke several times in the night, wondering whether an avalanche would come down on us, whether the river would rise 20 feet, or whether the packed earth we were parked on was going to crumble gently into the river. When morning came and none of these things had happened, I learnt that the others had been wondering just the same things, though none of us had spoken.

The next three days were a struggle against the elements, at times grim, at others invigorating. Certainly, it was a time that I remember very distinctly, because that period, together with the three days I have just described, was the period in which I was really working at full stretch, using my physical and mental powers to the utmost. We were climbing steadily, from 4,000 feet at the bottom of the canyon to 7,500 feet, and as we climbed it grew colder. There were very few towns marked on the map, and those were small, so we weren't quite sure what to expect each day. A further unknown factor was the altitude—although we weren't going very high, we would reach the height of Mexico City, where the altitude had caused considerable distress to Olympic competitors in the more prolonged events. At least the effects, if any, would be diminished by the fact that I was walking.

I set out before breakfast on Monday, May 6th, determined to get as many miles as possible in before sunset. The previous week's efforts had totalled only 230 miles, whereas I needed to do 300 a week to achieve my target. I did four miles before breakfast, stopping only for a word with the Arizona Highway Patrol. Out in the hills, with miles to the next town and very little traffic about, they were naturally curious about what I was doing, on foot and apparently alone, but when I explained they wished me luck. I walked for a further eight hours that day and managed to cover between 31 and 32 miles—a pace of 3-5 mph. It was cloudy and windy all day; I wore tracksuit trousers, sweater and a water and windproof anorak, plus my boots, and carried my walking stick, which I had learnt to use quite effectively. I walked through wooded country, seeing very few people all day, I remember coming down to cross a bridge over a creek at Carizzo, with the wind funnelling down the valley and almost blowing me off balance.

As I got higher the trees became sparser, though higher up still I came to a pinewood zone. In the afternoon I travelled a wild heathland, crossed by ravines and curiously pitted. The rain was being driven across it in grey sheets, and I was grinding along in a mood of dogged determination, when I saw the smoke of a fire just off the road. As I passed it, I saw two Native Americans standing beside the fire, under a tree. When I got downwind of them, I heard a strange sound, a sort of droning chant, punctuated by strange yelping shouts. I never worked out what they were doing, whether it was a religious ceremony, a drunken sing-song or something on their transistor radio.

At the end of the day I came to the pinewood zone, which reminded me of a rather dull part of Norway—a straight road, overhanging trees and the occasional wooden house. I tried a few paces jogging, and didn't feel a lot of pain, which was encouraging. I finished just before dark—I remember seeing the lights of the MGB parked under the trees. It wasn't a big day's mileage, but I felt satisfied that I was getting the better of my infirmities.

We stopped that night in the little town of Show Low. This name derived from an argument over some land, which had been settled by cutting a deck of cards. It was a one street town, a row of motels and stores. We stayed in a trailer park-cum-motel, where I was able to get a hot shower, the first since Superior, four days before. After walking all day, instead of running, I didn't feel too tired, and I went off with Maury to one of the two local radio stations. A young man in a hut beneath the mast appeared to run the whole thing single-handed—he put on a tape of music while he interviewed us, which he did most efficiently.

When we came out of the hut and stumbled across the rough field to our car the air was already very cold, and during the night it dropped to 28°. Back in the caravan it was warm and snug, and Sue had a lovely hot meal ready for us. There is no greater pleasure than sitting down after a hard day's work to satisfy a healthy appetite. It is the joy of a form of life that is simplified down to the physical essentials—run, eat, sleep. We had a gas heater in the caravan, which Mark got going, so it was very cosy, with the gas light glowing above us, as we sat over our coffee and discussed the day. I had for the time being forgotten the schedule and was only concerned with getting in as many miles as possible without aggravating my injury.

Sue and Mark had a mild argument about nothing very much, Maury went back to sleep in his camper, where he nearly froze, as he had neither heater nor sleeping bag. From that day on his enthusiasm for the outdoor life seemed to abate, and he spent more time in motels.

I had 13 miles to cover from last night's stop to Show Low and I thought I would try it in my running shoes, which should give me enough support to walk on, and would permit me to run a bit as well. It was still cold when I got on the road, so I kept my tracksuit on. I walked for the first mile, and my ankle didn't feel too bad, so I tried a bit of jogging. This was not so easy, but I evolved a method of progression which was quite fast, and within tolerable limits of discomfort—I put most of the weight on my left leg, and took only a short stride with my right; by swinging my foot out to the side more and not putting my heel on the ground I managed to avoid flexing the damaged right ankle. Whenever the pain increased, I would walk for a few minutes; at times I would do five minutes' walk, followed by five minutes' shuffle.

As I approached Show Low things improved, and I was able to jog the last three miles, getting in at 10.30. I had thought that this stage might take me four hours, based on yesterday's progress, so covering it in two-and-a-half was most satisfying. Maury had the man from the other radio station waiting to do an interview, so I was able to satisfy him, have a cup of coffee and a rest, get a hot shower and put on dry kit before going on. The rain which had been falling spasmodically during the morning had stopped; my ankle felt better, and I wanted to get 40 miles in that day. I ran for another nine or ten miles before lunch, across a rather featureless plateau. Most of it was grassland, there were few trees here, the land rose gradually to over 7,000 feet, with a few higher hills in the distance. These were covered by snow, and when the clouds came down again it was obvious that we too were above the snow line.

The first snow started to fall just after I had set out on my afternoon stage. I put my full tracksuit on, and that was soon covered with snow-flakes; still, it was not really cold, and running keeps one very warm—it was certainly easier than running in 90° heat. I got another ten miles done in an hour-and-a-half before stopping for tea. I dried off, changed and enjoyed my tea, while the snow got thicker, whirling around us and blotting out the view. Just as I was thinking of going out again, Mark came back down the road from Springerville, with a great bunch of letters from home. It was marvellous to feel back in touch with our family and our friends. I even had a letter from the girls in my form at school. One becomes so absorbed in one's own little world that it is hard to believe that any other world exists. It was amusing, too, because they were commiserating with us about the heat problem, and here we were in a snowstorm. They did tell us that our departure from Los Angeles had got plenty of publicity at home, which helped me to face the snow again. I put on my anorak and went on, keeping my head down to avoid getting snow in my eyes. It was a good thing that traffic was scarce in this part of the country. My leg was beginning to hurt again, but I managed to keep going with my limping shuffle, as I wanted to get my 40 miles in for the day.

Sue and Mark went off to Springerville to find a stopping place, but Maury had already booked into a motel, so they parked there—a good thing, in view of the weather. My 40 miles took me to the highest point on that stretch of road, over 7,000 feet up, Fortunately the snow stopped for the last few miles, but I felt pretty tired; the awkward gait, having to concentrate on every stride instead of running freely, had had its effect on me, and there may have been an altitude effect as well. I was very glad to reach the summit, climb into the car and be driven down to Springerville, 200 miles away. It may not have had much to offer in the way of culture or architecture, but there was a nice hot stove in Maury's motel room. Once again, I could relax completely and let the others do the work.

Sue brought me dry clothes and gave my legs a rub. Maury cooked supper for us, some pasta with meat and tomato sauce. I think it was only coincidence that Sue was sick during the night, and luckily she recovered quickly. Clive had not been quite himself during the day and was rather hot and feverish-looking the next morning. I thought it might just be an altitude effect; we dosed him with aspirin and kept him as quiet as possible.

On the morning of May 7th, I started off 20 miles west of Springerville. I wanted to run the whole distance to the motel, so left my tracksuit in the car when I got out, as I knew that I would get pretty hot after a few miles running. It was not snowing any more, but what I had not taken into account was the wind. It was blowing very strongly from the south-west and was freezing cold. My right leg was sore, and the muscles of my left leg were aching from all the extra work they had had to do the day before. If it had not been so cold, I would have walked for the first few miles to ease my legs, but I couldn't do that.

The road itself was downhill most of the way, which should have been an advantage, but in fact imposed extra strain, as I had to check myself from running too fast and increasing the trouble in my ankle. All I could do was keep going, trying to balance myself in the wind, trying to run fast enough to keep warm and not so fast as to worsen the injury. In fact, I really achieved none of these things. I was miserably cold, my muscles ached from the constant tension and my ankle hurt at every step. There was nothing to see except the road winding down across the desolate prairie. I think it was the worst time of the whole trip.

At times I shouted at the wind in my anger and frustration; at times tears poured down my face, and I longed to be back home. I thought of the warm bar of the White Hart in Wargrave; I thought of walking along the beach in Devon, running my toes through warm sand; I even thought of being back in the desert. There could be no question of giving up, no one was going to come out to me for two hours, and it was too cold to sit down and rest. There was nothing to do but curse and keep going, until at last it grew a bit warmer, and the pain in my ankle lessened. Sue brought me out coffee and biscuits, and I made my 20 miles in about three hours of running.

After this experience my nerves were pretty limp. Maury went off to drive to Albuquerque, as there was little PR work to be done out in the wilds. After I had showered and changed, I felt able to go on, so I put on warm clothing and my boots, and had a few miles easy walking before lunch. We still had the heater on in the caravan, because of the cold, and had hot soup at lunchtime. After lunch the snow closed down again, worse than the day before, and I had to wear two tracksuits as well as my anorak. On the other hand, I was warmer than in the morning, and my ankle was less painful. I walked for an hour, then jogged again for an hour before tea. It was 49 miles from Springerville to the next town, Quemado, so I obviously wasn't going to reach there that night. It looked as if we would have to go back to Springerville that night, but I sent Mark on ahead, just in case there was anywhere we could stay nearer at hand. To our joy he found a place, the Redhill Motel, only twelve miles ahead. I had done 24 miles in the morning and nine more since lunch. I decided to try and do at least another seven miles, which would get me 40 miles for the day.

Just after tea we crossed from Arizona into New Mexico. It was still snowing hard, and the snow almost obscured the Welcome sign, but soon after that it eased off. It was as if the gods had relented at last, after doing everything possible to prevent us leaving Arizona. We had been twelve days in the state, and during that time had endured the greatest extremes of weather as well as the worst injury of the whole trip. We had seen the most spectacular scenery; we had seen one of the most progressive cities as well as some of the most depressed country; and now, after almost a week of falling further and further behind the schedule, it looked as if our luck was beginning to turn. I reached 41 miles that day, only two miles from the motel, where we had hot baths and a drink.

There I learnt from Sue the last incident in our eventful crossing of Arizona. We had pulled into a lay-by for tea, and because of the snow had got stuck in the mud trying to get out of it. Luckily a local man came by with his pick-up truck and soon had them out. As they were preparing to drive away there was a low growl in the bushes. It was the nearest any of us ever got to a wild bear, butwe didn't stop to investigate! It was back to the warmth of the motel and the hope of a better day ahead.

Chapter 6
Across New Mexico

Our first morning in New Mexico dawned bright and clear, but also very cold. We had to scrape the ice off the car windows before starting. I did the couple of miles down to the motel before breakfast, and after that walked in my boots for an hour, as my ankle was still giving trouble. The sun warmed things up quickly, and we had a beautiful day, with the temperature in the sixties. Clive's feverishness had fortunately left him, so we were all in a more cheerful mood.

The morning passed quite uneventfully, and after I had covered 20 miles, partly jogging and partly walking, we stopped in a roadside rest area for lunch. In contrast to the previous three days at altitude it was warm enough to sit out at an outside picnic table. Just as we were in the middle of our lunch, a Highways lorry drew up. They didn't disturb us but proceeded to paint all the stones around the rest area, and the trash bin, in a bright yellow.

In the afternoon I again walked a good bit of the way. The land fell away from the plateau, through pine woods into a semi-desert area. At teatime I reached the town of Quemado—population (according to the sign): '250 good people and a few old crabs.' Quemado lies in a shallow valley, so that when you come down into it you can see the road winding through it and away into the distance. It is a long way from anywhere—70 miles to the nearest railhead they said, and it must have changed little since the days of the old West, except for the giant signs over the gas stations which reared up into the sky. The main industry was still cattle, Clive to his joy saw a 'real cowboy' riding a horse; the buildings were mostly unpretentious and white-painted; I noticed a few people glancing out of their windows, and there were a few men leaning up against the wall of the store, but being Westerners, they didn't even blink, let alone say anything. The only people who did talk to us during our tea stop were a very old man and some children.

The old man turned out to be a correspondent of Associated Press; he had been doing stuff for them for fifty years and so far as I could gather this was the most exciting thing that happened in Quemado since he had reported a hanging there 45 years before. The kids were interested and talkative. We were trying to find somewhere to stay that night and fixed on a point marked on the map as Omega. Two of the boys ran on ahead of me, to ask their parents to phone Omega for us, and after my usual half hour's break was up, I too set out.

On the way out of Quemado there was an old Spanish-style church, and behind that the graveyard. The climate here does not support much grass, so the graveyard was just a fenced-off area of dust. Wooden crosses stuck into the sandy soil leaned this way and that. It seemed to sum up the hardness of life in these remote areas. There was no concrete camouflage to stand between man and reality, just the mountains firm against the sky, the cattle grazing on the uncertain grass, and those crosses in the dust.

The end of the day was a long time coming for me. My ankle was hurting again, so just out of Quemado I changed into my boots and set off to walk the remaining ten miles to Omega. Since we had altered our watches by an hour on entering New Mexico I had plenty of daylight, and I found the walking pleasant. The gradient was slightly upwards, but not too much. The sun fell warm on my back and lit up the rolling grassland. I could see for several miles ahead of me, and there was little sign of life. Mark came back to say that there was nothing at Omega—the place was up for sale and there was no one about—so I decided to stay in Pie Town, the next village on the route. Just at eight o'clock I completed 40 miles for the day, and as I reached Mark's car a carload of people drew up to ask for my autograph; we got them to sign the witness book in return, and then bombed along the road to Pie Town.

Pie Town was not as big as Quemado, but it stood close to the Continental Divide, and boasted an Indian Trading Post, which was advertised on billboards for miles along the highway in either direction. There was no motel or trailer park, so we made our camp on the grass verge, opposite one of the petrol stations. We were in fact fairly self-sufficient, needing only toilet facilities, which the gas station possessed. On the front of the caravan was the bottle of propane gas which provided both light and heat, and we also had an insulated bag for ice and drinks tied on there. We had plastic water containers, a two-burner stove and an ice box. As long as we could refill with water, ice and food once a day we needed nothing else. Our rubbish we put into the heavy brown paper bags that our groceries came in, and we dumped these at the first trash bin. To give ourselves a little extra space we had a folding table and a set of camp stools, which we had packed in the boot of the MGB. For a night's stop such as the one in Pie Town I would sit out on one of the stools and sponge down my feet and legs in cold water, Sue would give my calf muscles a bit of massage, and then I would change into ordinary clothes for the evening meal.

Maury was still enjoying the fleshpots of Albuquerque that night, so we were on our own. Sunset was about 9 pm, and soon after that it got quite cold again. There was little traffic on that road, but we were serenaded by one of the local dogs, until Mark went out with Clive's baseball bat and threatened to smash its head in! We were up soon after seven as usual, and while we were finishing breakfast a reporter turned up to see us. He drove me back to the point ten miles west where I had stopped the night before, and I jogged back into Pie Town at about ten o'clock. From there it was only a mile or so to the Continental Divide, where we stopped to take pictures. As a physical feature it was rather disappointing—just a gentle slope on either side, but to me it signified a lot—the end of running at altitude, and the end of the mountains, with the strains which they imposed. From then on, the land sloped gently downwards to the East Coast, 2,000 miles away, with only the Appalachian range in between.

The first few miles after that sloped downhill, through valleys planted with pine trees, so that the air had a gorgeous smell after the rather arid plateau. We stopped for lunch after I had done 21 miles, then continued for the next town, Datil. We had expected this to be pronounced in the Spanish way, with a long 'a' in the first syllable, but we discovered that the natives pronounce it so as to rhyme with Seattle. It was a crossroads, a gas station and not much else. It was perhaps evidence of the relative poverty of this area that the land would only support one hamlet of this size every 40 miles. There had been a time when Datil had been a link on the cattle trail that led to Magdalena, there was an excellent camp site just outside the town, beside the wells that had first led to the building of a village in that spot. We decided to follow the example of the cattlemen and make our night's stop at Datil Wells.

As it was a Friday, I had to send my weekly piece off to *The Observer*. I had had plenty of time to think about what I was going to say, during my long hours of plodding, so it didn't take long for me to dictate it and for Sue to type it out, but despatching it was another matter, and Mark had to drive over 60 miles to Socorro to reach a Western Union office. It was always strange to think that on Sunday our family would be sitting at their breakfasts reading about it and sharing what we had been experiencing thousands of miles away.

Meanwhile I had to run the last stage of the day; I had already done 31 miles, so had a good chance of getting beyond the 40 which had been my quota for most of the week. A lot depended, of course, on whether I was walking or running. Walking, I would average 4 mph, so twelve miles would take me three hours. Running, even with a limp, would mean 8 mph, and therefore one-and-a-half hours for twelve miles. It was no good going on till I felt tired, because I felt tired after 30 miles, so each day I would fix a target, based on my physical condition and what I felt I needed to do, and try and get as close to it as possible. After three days at 40 miles I wanted to get back to my scheduled 43 miles a day.

The road out of Datil led on to a straight level stretch 35 miles long, without a turning until it reached Magdalena, and it was down this stretch that I plodded at the end of the day. My ankle was starting to hurt again, but by shuffling along with very short steps I could minimise the pain. At the beginning of this long straight was a series of mile posts, used for motorists to check their speedometers, which provided me with a welcome diversion. I timed myself over each mile, and though I could not run continuously, I managed to keep up between nine and ten minutes for each mile. By concentrating on a mile at a time, and then on the next one, I managed to cover my twelve miles in a bit under two hours; it was pretty miserable going compared with my road racing days, when I could run at exactly twice that speed, but at that time I was thankful just to keep getting in the miles.

The Datil Wells camp site was a beautiful spot. Maury had doubled back from Albuquerque, and we all had supper together, at a table outside in the evening sun. Sue produced pork chops with apple sauce and vegetables, which went down very well. The only drawback with camping out is the lack of a hot shower, which can be important when one is nursing an injury. The following morning, I found that my right ankle had swollen up, and that the Achilles tendon was thick and lumpy. This was a new development, and not a welcome one. It was clear that by limping with my right leg, and not putting my heel on the ground, I had put too much strain on the tendon. Disappointing as this was, I knew that wearing boots would take the strain of the tendon, as I had had this kind of injury before. It just meant more walking, and more patience. I cut back my daily target to 40 miles again—this would mean ten hours of walking, and at least twelve hours a day on the road, including rest stops.

With this in mind I got on the road at eight sharp the next morning. Ahead of me was another 23 miles of dead straight road, disappearing into a frieze of blue hills. Behind me were the higher hills I had come through, and either side of me the grassland stretched away like an ocean, with the occasional homestead floating boat-like on that vast expanse. Though I was walking and might well have felt frustrated at not being able to run fast along the level road, I felt peaceful—in that immensity of land and sky it was sufficient just to be part of it. My mind adjusted to the pace of the country, and as I moved slowly, slowly the folds of the hills altered their patterns, and slowly the shapes of clouds built up on the horizon.

After a whole morning I had covered 20 miles in five hours, and took my lunch-break, shorter than usual, just outside Magdalena. In the afternoon I walked through that town, once an important place. Once it was the goal of thousands of steers and scores of cowboys, the end of the Magdalena Trail, where the railroad started for the east. Now it is a dying town, shabby, unpainted, the home of people with not enough work, many of them depending only on the business brought by the passing motorist. There was a gem shop here, where Mark bought several specimens.

In Magdalena we met the mountains again, all through the day I had seen the cumulus clouds building up on the mountain tops, and now the sky was filled with them. There was a rumble, a flash of lightning, and soon I was in the middle of a terrific storm. I had nearly reached the point where the caravan was parked for tea, so I was able to shelter from the worst of it. I had managed an hour's jogging, which saved me a bit of time on my original estimate. Now I changed into my slacks, boots and anorak, and set off for another ten miles walking. The surroundings were very stimulating—a jagged ridge of mountains on my right, amid which the lightning flashed, with a wild scene of clouds filling the sky. Just at that time a television crew appeared, who had come down from Albuquerque to get some film. It was the first time we had had much attention since leaving Phoenix and it gave me a bit of a lift. I swung along the road at a steady 4 mph; later, when it was getting tedious, Sue joined me and walked for over an hour.

As we were getting close to Albuquerque, Maury had booked us in at a motel in Socorro. While I completed my 40 miles for the day, Clive was watching TV in the motel with Maury. Mark brought Sue up to walk with me, and then went up into the hills. We had seen a notice pointing to a laboratory, which was devoted to atmospheric studies; the topography of that area led to almost daily thunderstorms, which were studied by the laboratory, the only trouble was, he never managed to find the place.

By the time Sue joined me I was getting pretty fed up with walking. A couple of cars had stopped to ask if I wanted a ride, and one man had gone a little further, a car pulled up beside me and the driver beckoned me over; he was an old man with the seamed face of a farmer, and he had his wife with him. 'Me an' m'wife live up in the hills here', he said. 'We heard 'bout you comin' through.' He fished in his pockets. 'Here's a dollar; when you git into town go buy yourself some Sloan's Horse Liniment.' I thanked him warmly; it was a very kind thought, and I didn't get much in the way of encouragement on the road.

When I was getting bored, I tried estimating the distance between telegraph poles, timing myself on my wristwatch for ten poles distance and working it out on the basis of 4 mph, then I would try and walk faster for a stretch and improve my time for three poles distance. It wasn't really a very exciting game, so I was very pleased to have Sue walking with me for the last hour. I noticed that cars stopped more frequently when she was with me. The general run of the conversation was much the same: Driver: 'You wanna ride?' Walker: 'No, thanks, I'm walking.' Driver (with a laugh): 'You're walking for your health or sump'n?' Walker: 'No, I'm going from Los Angeles to New York, trying to break the record.' Driver (with a shake of the head): 'Well, the best of luck.' Still, it was human contact of a kind.

At last my 40 miles was completed, at about eight o'clock. Mark drove us the ten miles into Socorro, which was all downhill, as the town lies in the valley of the Rio Grande. On the way down we followed a pick-up truck being driven in the most erratic manner; whenever Mark tried to overtake it would swing. across to the middle of the road, then lurch in towards the ditch. We had been warned about drunk drivers, but this was the first example we'd had. We were greatly relieved to get down to the comfortable motel, after so many days in the wilds—however fine the scenery, there comes a time when the attraction of hot showers and clean sheets is very strong. Maury had got a meal ready for us, and even the TV programmes seemed tolerable for a while. We were visited by the local Schweppes bottler, Warren Schreiber, and his wife, and after the struggles of the past few days it seemed that we were a little less alone.

There were still the miles to be covered, though, and in the morning my ankle seemed to be worse than the day before, it was very swollen and puffy, and to get from the motel room to the caravan for breakfast I had to drag myself across the car park leaning on my stick. Maury saw me doing this and was horrified to think that I was about to embark on a 40-mile trek. He suggested that I took a day off. I knew however that the ankle would improve with exercise, as it had the day before. The puffiness was after all part of the healing process that had been going on during the night. I started out in my boots, the first quarter mile was very slow, with the stick taking a lot of the weight, then gradually I was able to walk more and more normally, until after half an hour I was striding along quite easily. I was able to move faster on the downhill and did the ten-and-a-half miles to Socorro in just under two-and-a-half hours. I had a break, and a drink, changed into running shoes and jogged through the town. Now we were out of the mountains it was warmer, but not hot, as we were still over 4,000 feet up. This is an area with a large Spanish-Mexican population, which was reflected in the style of the buildings as well as in the faces of the children who watched me go past. It was Sunday morning, the 11th of May, and the town was peaceful in the morning sun. As I came down the hill into the town, I had heard the distant call of the train coming up the valley, miles before it reached the town.

Crossing the mountains, I had been travelling due east, but here I had to turn north up the valley before reaching the next easterly road at Bernardo. The road here was Route 85, running up to Albuquerque, and for most of the way it was major highway, which I wasn't keen to run on. I was sorry to leave the quiet, narrow Route 60—by contrast the great double strip of concrete seemed unfriendly. There was plenty of room to run, with a shoulder, but it was fenced off from the country on either side of it, and the vehicles travelled very fast. I had a bit of diversion before lunch when another TV car came down and filmed me. Maury was taking pictures too, with a camera he had been given, as he wanted publicity pictures of the cars and the caravan, but I wasn't very optimistic of the results;

for one thing the shutter didn't seem to be working properly, and for another he was taking the pictures crouched down in front of me, and therefore directly at the sun which was just over my head.

It had been a slow sort of morning, with several delays—I ran for a while on a frontage road, but it petered out, and I had to climb over a lot of barbed wire to get back to due main road. It was getting hot and my leg was hurting, so I decided to stop after 20 miles. My estimate and Mark's differed for once, and I had to go on a mile further than I thought before reaching the caravan. It is surprising how short the distance is from mere tiredness to real distress—as long as I could think that the session was nearly over I was able to put up with the increasing heat and fatigue, but when the caravan failed to appear, and I could see a long stretch ahead of me I began to worry about my state and to feel thirsty. Ten minutes later I was inside the trailer enjoying a cool drink, but those ten minutes were really quite uncomfortable. At times like this I wondered more than ever at Don Shepherd's feat—how had he been able to manage, going for perhaps 20 miles without relief? I suppose the answer must be that one's estimate of what is tolerable depends as much on external conditions as on one's physical state. If you thought that you were going to get a drink after a five-mile run, and it wasn't available till after seven miles you would start to feel bad, whereas if you knew beforehand that there wouldn't be a drink until ten miles, you would be in a much better state at seven miles. As the Goons used to say: 'It's all in the mind, you know!'

Our mid-day stop that afternoon was on a frontage road, with Route 85 on our left, and the Rio Grande a few hundred yards away on our right. The river here had nothing grand about it at all. On either bank were masses of scrubby trees, there seemed to be none of the irrigation one might expect near such a large body of water. There was a straggle of buildings along the valley, but few of them looked very prosperous, the main crops seemed to be chickens and large families. At the place where we stopped was an old bar, with its paint peeling, its door boarded up, and glassless windows making hollow black spaces in the walls. There were empty beer bottles lying among the stones.

I continued up this dry valley for the whole of the afternoon. I walked for the first hour after lunch, then jogged for another hour. The country on either side had become sandy desert, split now and again by creeks coming down from the mountains to the west of me. As I walked, I could see the thunderclouds building up once more over these mountains, preparing to enact like repertory players their drama of yesterday afternoon. In my valley the sun still shone brightly, and I wished for the cloud to spread a little further over to give me shade. Every few miles up the road the state had thoughtfully provided rest areas, and I decided to stop for tea in one of these; the others went on to get it ready, and when I arrived, I found a conference in progress.

At the other end of the rest area a man was lying, apparently drunk; what were we to do about him? Sue and Mark had looked at him; he was asleep on the sand, in the hot sun; he had an empty gin bottle beside him, and his face was covered in sand. Several cars had stopped, looked at him and driven on, but Sue couldn't do that. What if he died through lack of attention? Clive was horrified by the whole thing—it was something he had not come across in the sheltered world of the Thames Valley. We took a sponge and bucket of water over to him and had a close look; he was breathing heavily but seemed all right except for some ugly bruises on his ribs and back, which were visible because his shirt was lying beside him. I lifted his head clear of the sand by tucking his shirt underneath him. I woke him, with some trepidation, and he gazed at me with the bleariest, most bloodshot pair of eyes I have ever seen. His face was blotchy, lined with little red veins, covered with sand, and at some time in his career his nose had been broken. We asked if he needed anything; he didn't. A drink? A sponge? 'Nah.' Where was he going? 'El Paso' (200 miles away). Was he all right? ''m awrigh'. You awrigh'?' There seemed to be nothing we could do, so we returned, thankfully, to our cup of tea and strawberry jam sandwiches.

The last part of the day I walked; it was boring; the road was straight, cars roared past on the way home to Albuquerque. It was odd to see amid this completely arid country car after car go by towing boats, but it turned out that there had been a water carnival on a lake further down the river. We got accustomed to the fact that people living 100 miles from a river would own a boat and trail it over at weekends, a tribute not only to the material wealth of many Americans but also to their enterprise. To my relief the distance to Bernardo turned out to be a mile shorter than I expected, and we made camp there for the night. What we thought was at least a village turned out to be just a gas station, but there was nothing else for many miles ahead, as we were turning east once more, on the minor Route 60.

We found a place where we could pull off the road, got water from the gas station, and lit a camp fire to cheer ourselves up. Maury had had some compelling business in Albuquerque, so was not with us. I had only done 38 miles that day, but I decided to stop at the point where we had pitched camp and make an early start the next morning. As we were not far from Albuquerque (45 miles), Sue and Mark took the opportunity to drive up there and go to a movie—it was the only chance since leaving Los Angeles. While they were away, I had a visit from the family who lived at the gas station—shy, dark-eyed little girls.

I got my early start in the morning, crossing the various channels of the Rio Grande and walking up a gentle slope towards the hills on the eastern side of the valley. It was delightfully peaceful to be back on Route 60 again-we saw very few vehicles all day. When I started running, I put a Scholl heel pad under my right heel—I had found these to be useful in past cases of Achilles strain—and found my running that day much easier than the day before.

By the mid-morning break we were getting into the hills again, and at the end of the day I reached Mountainair, over 6,000 feet up. My clearest memory of the day is of looking across the prairie towards the railroad, three or four miles away. At this distance the train looked like a toy, crawling up a long green slope towards a tunnel in the hills, but in the silence the sounds carried very clearly-the throb of the four diesel engines, the rattle of the great string of trucks, and occasionally that most nostalgic of sounds, the deep wailing whistle. After I had followed the road up a winding climb of a few hundred feet, it turned back on itself and crossed the cutting of that railroad. Even nowadays it is a pretty remote area; goodness knows what it was like when that cutting was blasted out of the rock, forging another link in the country's lifeline. For many days thereafter we ran close to the railroad, sometimes too close for convenience, but we never failed to be impressed by the trains.

It was a day of little incident—Maury returned from town and had another go at taking pictures. In the afternoon he decided to go ahead to Santa Rosa—120 miles—leave the films and double back to us again. On the road to Mountainair I met a pleasant woman with two little girls, who gave us a bundle of fresh spinach from her garden. The leg trouble seemed to be receding, but it was still a bit painful on the way up to Mountainair. For the last five miles Mark came out and ran with me; we went right through the town, past our camp, which was in a rest area on the east side of town, and a further three miles beyond, giving me an encouraging 43 miles for the day.

I was still pretty tired and felt a bit disappointed that I was not getting used to the work as quickly as I had hoped—I had been going three weeks now. Sue pointed out, though, that it was the first time for over a week that I had been running for most of the day rather than walking.

In the evening we were pleased to see the Schreibers again. As well as bringing down some mail for us, Mrs Schreiber had made us a chocolate cake, which we appreciated very much. The site of our camp was exposed to a rather chilly wind, so I just had a quick sluice down and hopped back into the caravan, where Sue had one of her risottos ready. Just as we had decided that Maury wasn't going to find us, because it was getting dark, he roared up, and just had time to bolt his risotto before taking me into Mountainair to put through a call to the Canadian Broadcasting Corporation in Toronto. We had to find a call box and get through before they went off the air, but after a bit of dashing about he found a telephone in a garage.

At the back the proprietor was playing poker with three friends—oldish men in overalls, with wrinkled country faces, they paid little attention to our phone call, just kept on with the casual ritual of their game; how many nights had those men played cards together at the back of the garage in that little town, and are they still playing? How little the pattern of our lives is affected by 'important' things, as opposed to the gradual accumulation of trivia, in the way that the course of a river is affected by the slow silting up of the bed over many years.

The morning of May 13th was a good one, with a warm sun and a bit of following breeze. I walked for the first hour and jogged for the second, which took me into Willard, a sleepy little town. The lack of pressure on space gives these American towns a character totally unlike anything found in Europe; there must be a connection too with the security in which these towns have grown up. I know that they have had their Indian wars and the occasional bandit, but they have not experienced the centuries of strife that have been the lot of every country in Europe baron against baron, Norman against Saxon, Frank against Hun or Magyar against Turk. In Europe the houses huddle together for protection; the tilled fields run to the back doors, in places where each acre is precious. Out in the West the houses and the stores stand back from the road, with empty space around each one. The town is wide open to friend and foe alike, there are no gates to be shut. Something of the same sort is found in the people of these places; they mind their own business, but they are friendly and open, without guile or suspicion. One feels that there are few secrets.

It was another 35 miles to the next village, Encino, across the same empty plateau of grassland that we had crossed the day before. I ran parallel to the railroad the whole way, and this provided the only distraction for my thoughts. I was able to run for the rest of the morning, but walked for an hour after lunch, as a safety precaution. My ankle had almost returned to its normal shape and was giving me little trouble. For the first mile of my afternoon walk Clive came with me, skipping along in and out of the grass, stopping to pick up interesting bits of debris and then dashing after me again. After this it became a habit for him to walk a mile a day with me, it gave us a chance to talk about things, which I didn't feel like doing in the evenings. He was particularly interested in the animal life, and we often came across dead animals on the road, particularly snakes.

As Clive had walked with me, and Sue had done a bit of running with me at times, Maury thought he would have a go at running some of the way. Sue tried to dissuade him, but of course this only put him on his mettle, towards the end of the afternoon, therefore, having taken the other vehicles on to Encino, they all came out in Maury's camper. I suggested that Sue took the camper on not more than a mile-and-a-half, as it was Maury's first attempt. Wearing shirt, shorts and a pair of Adidas shoes he'd borrowed from Mark, he launched himself from the camper as I ran past. I was on a down-slope at the time, and as we came to the dip at the bottom, before the next rise, I thought: 'I'd better take it easy to the top of this hill.'

As we started the upgrade Maury started puffing heavily, and eventually gasped out: 'You go on, Bruce,' and stopped. He had only managed a quarter of a mile from the caravan. I'm afraid that Sue and Mark absolutely fell about with laughter. To Maury's credit, he got jogging again at the top of the hill and completed the mile-and-a-half. I think that he had been deceived by the apparent ease with which I moved at 8 mph, forgetting that my body after years of training was virtually a running machine.

We got to Encino at about seven o'clock, Mark running the last four miles with me, and received a quite unexpected and very heartening welcome. Sue had found a nice trailer park, with both a shower and an electric hook-up, and when I arrived, I found a large group of boys from the local high school gathered round, and a photographer with an odd accent, who turned out to be their teacher. He was a small man, with a brusque, volatile, wise-cracking nature; when he was taking pictures, I thought he was just a rather pushy press man, but then he introduced himself, and the boys with him.

And so we met Victor Amballos, a.k.a. Victor the Greek—probably the most remarkable character of the entire journey, certainly the most extrovert. If ever anyone was all things to all men, it was Victor. He was an enthusiast about everything. He introduced his boys, speaking to them in Spanish, which he had just taught himself; most of them were members of the basketball team of which he was the coach. His main line was teaching biology, but he had other reasons for being out here, teaching in an educationally deprived area and discovering a new part of the United States.

Victor invited us over to his house for the evening, we met his wife, son and daughter, and learnt a lot about New Mexico. He produced, to Clive's delight, several live rattlesnakes in jars, the first live rattlers we'd seen. He woke them up and banged the sides of their jars until they rattled furiously and struck against the sides. He gave Clive a live horned toad, and a book about the fauna of the south-west, and he showed us his gem collection. He and his wife were what they call 'rock buffs'. They both collected semi-precious stones and made them into jewellery with their own cutting and polishing tools. Not only did they show us their work, but they presented us with an assortment of stones—moss agate, tiger eye, garnet, 'wonderstone' and 'apache tears', all found in New Mexico—as well as some lovely polished coral and an African amethyst. We finally got to bed at 11.30 after a most interesting evening.

In the morning the boys came out to see me off as I set out in my boots for the first hour's walking. Yesterday's stage had been 45 miles, the best day since leaving Phoenix on April 30th. The previous week had been only 270 miles, a further loss of 30 miles on top of the distance I had lost before, and there was a strong temptation to push on as far as possible, now that I was recovered, but I resisted it. I knew that too much exertion would only lead to recurrence of the injuries; the thing to do was to build up gradually, and for the time being 45 miles a day was quite enough.

In fact, as I was 100 miles behind my target, with 45 days to go—an extra two miles per day was all that I needed.

There was no sign of life from Maury until just before 8.30, when I left; obviously the previous day's effort had been too much for him—he was normally up and about long before I was. My leg seemed much better, and in spite of the late start I made 22 miles before lunch. The morning run took me through Vaughn, a long town winding along the highway, where a lot of people came out to give me a shout; from there we took Route 54 up towards Santa Rosa, the point at which our route joined Route 66.

The afternoon went equally well, and after my hour's walking I was running quite briskly. For most of the previous few days I had been going for three miles at a stretch between drinks, and those three miles had been taking me 24 minutes; now I was doing them in 22 or even 22 minutes, so I switched over to doing four miles at a go, taking about half an hour each. I managed to get my 45 miles in in good time and finished up ten miles from Santa Rosa. Maury caught up with us in the afternoon but this time he didn't volunteer to run with me.

Santa Rosa was larger than anything we'd seen since Socorro; we stayed in a cheap motel, and Sue caught up with the washing and ironing. We tried some enchiladas for supper, which were good, but a bit hot, so we had watermelon afterwards to cool us down. The run at last seemed to be becoming more of the steady day's work I had hoped it would be, and less of a traumatic struggle with myself. The next day started off well enough. I did the ten miles into Santa Rosa before the morning break, and then set out on Route 66.

Route 66 is one of the great highways of America. The twin ribbons of concrete flatten the hills and span the rivers to easily that the motor-bound man loses the sense of change that is the essence of travel. To the traveller on foot this type of route is very boring, and it engenders a state of mind that would probably have a medical name if it was common enough. One is cut off from the country around one, and the only thing that has reality is the thundering traffic; as one becomes more tired, the noise and buffeting of the passing trucks becomes less and less tolerable; when you rest in the caravan it is not much better; unless you can get off on to a frontage road each truck sucks at the little trailer and then rocks it back with a great on rush of oil-laden air.

The only thing at all memorable that day was the place we stopped for lunch—a mock-up row of Western old-time stores, with peacocks wandering about in the car park. Towards the end of the day I got more than usually tired, due possibly to the boredom, and the fact that I was on my own for quite a long time while the others were looking for a place to stay the night. My thoughts, which during the day had ranged over a number of topics, narrowed down to the concentration on miles and minutes, my pace altered little, though I was becoming more and more tired and thirsty, I would look at my watch and work out how much longer I had to go on running, then stare into the distance or count footsteps, trying to take my mind away from the slow passage of time. I had been reading *Catch* 22 and one of the characters in that used to seek out the most boring occupations in order to make his life seem longer; the last hour of that run seemed like a day to me.

At last I saw the MGB appearing ahead of me, Sue brought me a drink and Mark got out and ran with me, I managed to do my 45 miles, and was able to run right into our camp, at the back of a store and filling station, in a spot called Montoya. There was no hook-up or shower, but it was convenient, and in any case, Maury was not with us, having gone on ahead to Amarillo. The films which he had had developed in Santa Rosa had been a washout, so he was going to get a professional to take some pictures.

When we joined Route 66, we had also joined the route taken by the pioneers of 1928, in their 'Bunion Derby', and in the store in Montoya we met for the first time one of the people who had seen them come through— the old man who kept the store. He had been keeping the store in 1928 too and remembered well how they looked: 'They were an untidy lot, like a lot of tramps; they didn't care 'bout anything, just come in, buy a can o' beans an' eat 'em straight outta the can, then off they'd go again.'

In the morning I did my now customary hour's walk, and when I started running, I took out the heel pad, as I didn't want to become dependent on it, and felt that my tendon could do without it. My leg was all right, but for some reason I felt very depressed. It may have been what I called 'freeway neurosis', engendered by the impression that one is always in the same place, or it may have been due to the head wind; on the other hand it might have been due to some physical condition. At break time I took a vitamin and iron tablet, more for luck than anything else. Whatever the cause of the trouble was, I felt quite cheerful in the afternoon. It was Friday now, the day for sending off my *Observer* piece, and at last I was able to send a fairly encouraging report home. My leg had improved, I had gone 45 miles for the last three days, and, even more important, I clocked up that day my thousandth mile of running since leaving Los Angeles. At the time I wrote:

> *The boost to our morale of having those four figures on the scoreboard on the side of our caravan is tremendous. After what seems like ages of nibbling at the fringes of the journey, we have now taken a great chunk out of it.*

I had 1,000 miles behind me, and the Texas border was only a few miles ahead, but, as happened in Arizona, there was a little surprise in store for us before I made it to San Jon, our last overnight stop in New Mexico. I had sent off the piece from Tucumcari, where we had stopped at mid-day, and mentioned the good running conditions I had enjoyed for most of the week, I should have known better! During the lunch break the wind increased and clouds moved up. It grew colder, and we heard typhoon warnings for West Texas and for our area.

After lunch I was all right for about half an hour, though the wind was blowing strongly from the north. Then I saw that the sky ahead of me had a reddish colour, caused by clouds of dust blowing from the fields; to the north-east I could see grey rain squalls moving towards me. The wind got up even more, and backed round a bit, so that I had it on my shoulder; I was running faster now than at any time for weeks, with big raindrops scudding past me. The caravan had stopped a mile up the road, and it became a race between me and the storm. I got within about 600 yards of it when the storm broke over me, and though I covered the ground at a brisk scuttle I was soaked when I leapt inside. I dried off, and we watched the storm raging across the open country, with hailstones rattling on the highway. As it showed no signs of letting up, we took an early tea. By this time, it struck none of us as incongruous to be having tea and fruit cake, in the middle of a hailstorm, on Route 66, USA.

The storm stopped; I started; after my soaking I didn't feel like doing a lot more, but I added ten miles to the 33 I had already done, and finished up five miles short of San Jon. That night we had hot baths in the San Jon Motel, dined off steak and that fresh spinach, and slept soundly, looking forward to the following day, when we would enter the Lone Star State.

Chapter 7
Across Texas to Oklahoma

The morning of May 17th was damp and rather chilly; the storm of the day before had cooled things down a lot. I did the five miles into San Jon without trouble, but between there and the Texas border a new trouble arose. I had gone about three miles from the motel when I began to get a pain in my left hip; from a dull ache it quickly became painful, so that I had to walk for a while; even the walking caused a bit of pain, and I immediately began to fear the worst. The pain felt deep down in the hip, probably in the ball and socket joint itself; I supposed that the days of limping had warped my frame, as it were, and the cold wet weather had brought about this painful friction in the joint.

My reaction to situations like this is to envisage the worst possible result, and then consider what should be done. I got in eleven miles before breakfast, rested, and had some massage on the hip. When I got going again it gave no trouble for three miles, then gradually got worse; I found that if I took very short strides, raising my knees very little and therefore rotating the hip very little, then it was fairly comfortable. The only trouble was the strain of keeping my body braced upright, while shuffling along with these tiny paces. I carried on down the road with the gait of an old man, the kind one sees coming in ten minutes behind the field in a club road race. Was this the four-minute miler, the man who demolished the opposition in the European Games 5,000 metres? No matter, I was getting there. We lunched just west of the Texas border, and when I walked out of New Mexico into the fourth state on our journey, we had a little stop to take pictures.

The change on crossing into Texas was quite amazing, considering that the border is only a line on the map. The fact that the road changed from two lanes to four was understandable to us, having heard all about the way everything in Texas is bigger, but the abrupt change in the nature of the countryside was not expected. From a land of rather arid prairie we were suddenly in arable farming country, green and fertile-looking, with square fields bordered by irrigation ditches. The farmhouses as well as the fields looked more prosperous, they were neatly painted wooden houses, mostly white, or light grey with white woodwork, and they had green mown lawns and flower beds.

Texas is certainly a richer state, and at the time it was a warmer one. We had been losing height gradually ever since Mountainar; Tucumcari is 4,089 feet up, and Amarillo, then 70 miles ahead, is 3,664 feet. It grew quite warm that afternoon, in the seventies anyway, and this seemed to make my hip better. It was still a long day, though and by the time I reached Adrian, having done 45 for the day, I was very tired. The one thing which kept a spark of interest going was the presence of mile marker posts along the road. These had made their appearance when we reached the border, little white numbers on a green background. Their distance apart agreed precisely with the distances on our car milometers, so that I could say to Sue: 'Go on four mile posts', for the next drink stop. What is more, it gave me an interest in measuring my speed. It was from these that I confirmed my walking speed in boots to be exactly 4 mph. When I was running, I would try and keep up seven-and-a-half-minute miles, and then try to improve on them. After a break, when my hip was not troubling me, I could run at seven-minute miles, but at the end of the day I was happy to keep up eight-minute miles.

On crossing the border into Texas, we had crossed into another time zone, and were now three hours ahead of California time. For the purposes of our scoreboard, this meant that the mileage was calculated up to 1 pm each day. As I had started on Monday, April 21st, at 10 am, four weeks would be completed at 1 pm on Monday, May 19th. The accumulation of 45-mile days was by now making my average look a little better—it was now creeping up towards 41—and having done 1,000 miles gave me confidence. In the early stages the main interest was in our destination, which seemed rather improbable, now, the fact that I had run all the way from California was regarded as impressive in itself. Few people stopped on the big highway, but those who did were encouraging. Once a young Marine talked to me and gave me a drink, another time an old couple. Meeting people who genuinely admired what I was doing gave me the strength to go on, at times the interruptions were tedious, as I shall relate, but on the whole, they helped us.

The morning after leaving Adrian, a routine stop by the roadside without any special features, we met our first Texan. I was running along the frontage road, which parallels the highway all along that part of Route 66, and gives a welcome respite from main road name, a pick-up truck came cruising up alongside me and a man leaning bid me good morning. He was a cheerful middle-aged man, with his two sons in the cab beside him. He said: 'My daddy in Austin read you was comin' 'long this way; he rung me up and said to look out for you.' He asked some sensible questions about my routine, then turned off to his farm. Half an hour later he was back: 'Should be in church, by rights, but we reckoned we'd see how you was gettin' on.' We met him again the next day, and we exchanged addresses, to send Christmas cards. When people talk of 'Americans', and describe national traits, that is one of the men I shall think of, to think if the remarks fit. Compared to many farmers I have met in England, his mind did not set boundaries; it is a country where all things are possible, where the country boy can imagine himself to be President, or to be an astronaut, and can make it.

The goal that day, Sunday 18th, was Amarillo, or to be more precise, a motel on the western edge of it, just 45 miles from Adrian. Maury had been doing his stuff in Amarillo in the previous couple of days, and we had two TV crews out to film us. We were getting used to this, but it always created a bit of diversion for me. They generally worked in pairs, with a flashy car, and, being young men, we could talk and laugh with them. They would film me coming down the road from a long way off, then film my face in close-up for agony shots, then my feet from various angles. If they wanted an interview, they would usually ask the same questions, to which I of course had the answers. 'Why are you doing this?' 'To get to the other side'. 'Do you have any special diet?' 'No, just food, and lots of it.' 'Have you had any interesting things happen to you?' 'What's been the toughest part?' and so on. I had a few frivolous answers, but most of the time I felt I had to play it straight. I felt reluctant to go deeply into what I felt about the run; I think this is an English characteristic—when we talk about serious things, we make a joke about them, and we talk very seriously and in detail about trivia, such as cars, weather and the best way to get to West Wittering.

I slogged on to Amarillo, on straight flat road. Down the road you can pick out the towns by the great concrete grain silos, standing beside the railroad and dwarfing the one-storey buildings in the same way that the great cathedrals of Europe must have dominated the shacks of the peasants who built them. At each road intersection the graceful concrete arch of a bridge gave me a momentary patch of shade and broke the otherwise endless road into sections of a more tolerable length. My friends the mile markers waited for me the whole way—trustworthy—and with their help, and of course Sue and Mark giving me drinks and sponges, I reached Bronco Lodge Motel by 6.30 pm There was a little gaggle of news people there, including two men from the *Amarillo Daily News*, with whom we had an interesting chat. I found the journalists we met were mostly intelligent and amusing company, with their breadth of experience they were able to make comparisons and to understand what I was talking about.

We had a good dinner—we thought we ought to enjoy a Texas steak while we were there—which was somewhat enlivened by the fact that we were in a 'dry' county. Maury had bought a bottle of wine before we left New Mexico, and the trouble we had drinking it made us feel we were back in the Prohibition days. The waitress ushered us into a separate room and insisted that we kept the bottle under the table; then she wanted to see our identity cards, which of course we didn't have. Anyway, it gave the meal a touch of excitement that was lacking in the food, however plentiful it was.

After putting Clive to bed we went out to a drive-in—a real treat for me, as I hadn't done anything like that in all my four weeks on the road. We went to see *2001: A Space Odyssey*; as the Apollo 10 rocket was at that moment on its way to the moon it was of more than usual fascination. The spaceman's experience must be unusually difficult to communicate—there is the fear of being largely unable to control what is happening to them, and the enforced detachment from their environment. For us on earth the detachment is even greater—we sit and watch on the TV or cinema screen pictures that are taken by automatic cameras and we cannot know what it is like to be up there; you would have to be inside that little room, with its metal, plastic and paint, conscious of the tons of fuel only a few feet away, conscious both of your loneliness and also of your utter dependency on the men who are down below. I often tried to feel myself in their position, as I plodded my way along the endless concrete strip, and my guess is that the thing that keeps them balanced is their close involvement with the ground operations; they are so used to working with the team, simulating the operations, sometimes for hours, and then walking out and having lunch with the controllers in the canteen, that this is just another, more prolonged, simulation; their capsule is part of the big machine in which they spend their working lives, and the chances of it going wrong are therefore pretty small. All this digression has nothing to do with my run, but my excuse for putting it in is this: every day people ask me questions, and the most common one was: 'What do you think about during all those hours?' That is one of many things, and there is enough in that theme for quite a lot of thinking.

Monday morning in Amarillo saw the beginning of the fifth week of the trip; it was a hectic day compared to the previous two weeks, and at the end of it I had decided that I much preferred the country to the city. We had come a little way off the main highway to the hotel, and I had to go through the business centre of the city for the benefit of the photographers. Other complications were that Mark had to get some things done to the MGB and Sue had to do some shopping for Clive's birthday presents.

Both cars had served us very well up to this point, but they had already done nearly 3,000 miles each in a great variety of conditions, and we owed it to ourselves as well as to the cars to make sure that minor troubles did not get a chance to multiply to a point at which they might interfere with the smooth progress of the run. We worked out a procedure: I was to run into the town centre straight after breakfast, and the others were to catch me up there, and rendezvous with the TV party, who wanted to do an interview. Mark was then to take due trailer 15 miles ahead, park it, and return to get the car serviced. After the TV interview Maury was to keep near me until Sue had done her shopping and caught me up again. It meant that all four of us had to have maps and know where I was likely to be at any stage of the morning.

It worked out reasonably well; there were a couple of periods when they seemed to have lost me, but they didn't last long. Mark got misdirected going out of town, and left the car on the wrong highway, which caused Sue a bit of frustration trying to find it, but luckily Mark got the car done and caught us up before I needed the trailer at lunchtime. The heat was pretty fierce, 94° by noon and reflecting off the new white concrete. The first part of the route out of Amarillo seemed to be all naked concrete, flyovers and underpasses, but no trees.

In spite of all this, and the worry of not being quite sure when I would get my next drink, I felt quite good; my tolerance of heat had obviously improved considerably since Phoenix. It was gone one o'clock when I stopped, having done 22 that morning. The best thing of the morning was passing a sign which read 'Oklahoma City 250 miles.' I had reached a stage now where 250 miles didn't sound much—only just over five days—and Oklahoma City was very near the halfway mark. It really gave me something to run for. If I did another 23 miles that day, I calculated, I just had to keep up 45 miles a day to reach Oklahoma on Saturday night, the 24th. As my schedule originally set me to reach there on the 23rd (allowing for the fact that I started two days later than planned), it meant that I was getting back on terms with it. These calculations could be made to last for several miles of running; about the middle of the morning my mind would start to run out of subjects which grew naturally out of the previous day and night's experience, and this was the easiest thing on which to fasten. First there was the total mileage up to 1 pm to work out; Sue or Mark would chalk this up on the side of the caravan. Then there was the overall average—this reached 41 miles per day on the first morning out of Amarillo, and should reach 42 by Oklahoma. More involved calculations followed—if I had gone 1,140 miles, then I had exactly 1,700 to run. What was the minimum daily mileage needed to beat the record? What was the most likely time, based on keeping up 45 a day, and what was the best possible time, based on getting to 48 or 50 a day? Every now and again something would distract me, and I would have to start again, so that this could keep me going for several miles, by which time I could start thinking about the lunch-break.

I finished up pretty tired that day—the effect of the heat seemed to catch up on me later in the day, or it may have been the late night, or the interruptions. Maury got a motel room in Groom, and we stayed in the caravan, but used his shower.

The next day he took off for Oklahoma City, notifying the local press on his way through the small towns, and didn't reappear till Thursday. It was extremely useful to us to have him doing all this work, though it meant more demands on me in the way of interviews. One expects this as the price of sponsorship; nevertheless, it cannot be denied that there was less friction when we were just the family group together. During periods of stress, and there were plenty of those, it helps not to have to go to great lengths to communicate one's thoughts and needs; Sue, Clive, Mark and I shared the same background and the same jokes, it wasn't necessary to spell everything out.

Transcontinental Run 1969
Los Angeles to New York

We, the undersigned, witness that **Bruce Tulloh**

left the City of Los Angeles	at 10^{AM} on 4-21-69	Signed	Ernest d Conway Exec. asst to the Mayor
arrived at passed through left	at (on	Signed	Jack Jack Schweppes Western States
~~arrived at~~ ~~passed through~~ ~~left~~ Ontario (Milliken r Mission)	at 6 40pm on April 21st	Signed	
~~arrived at~~ ~~passed through~~ left " "	at 720 a.m. on April 22nd	Signed	
arrived at ~~passed through~~ left Pedley "	8.05 a.m " at 9.10 a.m on "	~~Signed~~	interviewed by KPRO radio
arrived at passed through left Riverside (Van Buren r Arlington	at 9.35 on " a.m	Signed	

arrived at	Adrian, TEXAS	7.30 P.M.	MAY 17th	Signed	Adrian Service Center
passed through		at on			+ Trailer Park
left	"	8.25 A.M.	MAY 18th		N.C. Edmonds
arrived at	Amarillo, TEXAS	6.30 P.M.	MAY 18th	Signed	James D. Pratt
passed through	(Rancho Motel) at	on			KVII-TV Amarillo, Texas
left	"	9.05 A.M.	MAY 19th		
arrived at	4 m. W. of Groom, TEXAS	7.25 P.M.	MAY 19th	Signed	C. W. Lane
passed through	at	on			State Motel
left	" - - "	8.30 A.M.	MAY 20th		
arrived at				Signed	C. W. Lane
passed through	Groom, TEXAS	at 9.30 A.M. on	MAY 20th		State Motel
left					

arrived at 3 m. W. of Lela, Texas   7:30 A.M.   MAY 20th
passed through   at   on   MAY 21st
left   8:15 A.M.   MAY 21st
Signed   West 40 Camp Area / Gaye Nell Schlegel

arrived at
passed through   Lela, Texas   at 9:15 A.M. on MAY 21st
left
Signed   West 40 Camp Area / Gaye Nell Schlegel

arrived at   1 m. E. of Sayre, ~~Texas~~ OKLA.   6:40 P.M.   MAY 21st
passed through   at   on
left   1 m. E. of Sayre, OKLA.   8:40 A.M.   MAY 22nd
Signed   Richard L Barber / SAYRE POLICE P.D.
seen to leave by workmen at Sayre Park Campgrd.

arrived at
passed through   44/152 intersection, OKLA.   at 2:45 P.M. on MAY 22nd
left
Signed   Ronald McLaulie / Carrier Daily Mail. / Ronald K Hill

arrived at
passed through   Cordell, OKLA.   at 4:45 P.M. on MAY 22ND
left
Signed   Loftonian Lodge / Oris L. Lofton

arrived at   12 m. E. of Cordell, OKLA.   7:0 P.M.   MAY 22ND
passed through   at   on
left   8:40 A.M.   MAY 23rd
Signed   Loftonian Lodge / Oris L. Lofton

arrived at
passed through   8-281/152 Jct. OKLA.   at 4:25 P.M. on MAY 23rd
left
Signed   (illegible) / KOCO TV ABC TV / OKLA CITY, OKLA

arrived at   Salyer's Lake Park OKLA.   5:0 P.M.   MAY 23rd
passed through   at   on
left   5:15 P.M.   MAY 23rd
Signed   Salyer Lake Manager / Mrs Bethel Henderson

FINAL PLANS FOR ARRIVAL OF BRITISH RUNNER

BRUCE TULLOH IN NEW YORK, ON

COMPLETION OF HIS RECORD-BREAKING (66 DAYS) RUN

FROM CITY HALL, LOS ANGELES

Wednesday, June 25

Arrival at City Hall, NYC: 12 o'clock (Noon)

- Tulloh will approach the City from Staten Island the morning of June 25. He is scheduled to run aboard the Staten Island Ferry at the ferry slip in Staten Island at approximately 11:05 A.M. (This ferry will leave South Ferry for Staten Island at 10:40 A.M. All members of the press and others concerned with Tulloh's fantastic achievement might want to be on board.) The Department of Marine & Aviation has promised complete cooperation.

The crossing from Staten Island to South Ferry, Manhattan will take about 20 minutes, during which time Tulloh will jog on the deck.

11:30   :   The ferry will dock at South Ferry. Tulloh will run North on Broadway to City Hall. (The 3-car and trailer caravan that accompanied him on his transcontinental run will take another route -- suggest going North on Trinity Place and East to City Hall.) The NYC Police Dept. has assured traffic control for Tulloh at each cross-Broadway intersection so he won't have to stop.

12 Noon   :   Tulloh arrives at City Hall for official welcome and appropriate ceremonies. A request has been made for Mayor John V. Lindsay and Commissioner of Public Events John (Bud) Palmer to greet Tulloh, who is delivering to Lindsay a message from Mayor Sam Yorty of Los Angeles, in the interests of Anglo-American relations, the fact of his having broken by a week the previous record for this feat (73 days, set by South African Don Shepherd in 1964), the international interest and concern of press and people in Tulloh's achievement (among them Britain, Canada, France, Germany, Australia, etc.). Sir Anthony Rouse, British Consul General in New York, and other British officials, will be present, as will Commander Edward Whitehead of Schweppes (U.S.A.) Ltd., whose company is underwriting 116-lb. Tulloh's incredible attempt to break the record for the 2,850-mile run. Mrs. (Sue) Tulloh, and 7-year-old Clive Tulloh, both of whom accompanied the British track star the entire distance, will also be present. And Mark Alderson, Tulloh's 19-year-old cousin who drove one of the two British Leyland cars in the cross-country entourage.

Tulloh will receive mementoes from the City of New York at the brief ceremony on City Hall steps.

12:30 P.M. :   Caravan leaves City Hall, led by top-down convertible carrying Commander Whitehead and Bruce Tulloh, and including the two automobiles, a small caravans International trailer (in which the Tulloh family lived for the past 66 days since leaving Los Angeles City Hall at 10 A.M. on Monday, April 21), and the mobile press unit operated by Tulloh's manager Maury Soward for the entire trip.

1:00 P.M. :   Caravan arrives at Toots Shor's restaurant for
(THIS MEMORANDUM   welcoming and press luncheon, which members of the
IS YOUR INVITATION) press and others will attend by invitation. In addition to Bruce Tulloh, his wife, son and cousin, Mayor Lindsay, and other selected officials of the city government are invited, along with Sir Anthony Rouse, Consul General, and other officials of the British government, Commander Whitehead, and others who have helped make Tulloh's achievement possible.

~~arrived at~~ passed through Norristown ~~left~~	at 12:35 p.m. on June 23rd	~~Signed~~	interviewed by local press TV (Channel 3, Channel 16)
arrived at Buckingham, Pa. passed through " " left	6:20 p.m. June 23rd at 8:44 a.m. on June 24th	Signed	
arrived at crossed passed through Delaware River left	at 9:30 a.m. on June 24th	~~Signed~~	
~~arrived at~~ passed through New Brunswick N.J. ~~left~~	at 5:00 p.m. on June 24th	Signed	interviewed at Stephen's Barber Shop.
arrived at Ford, N.J. ~~passed through~~ left	6:10 p.m. June 24th at on June 25th	Signed	interviewed by local Press.
arrived at passed through Durnapple Blvd left & Richmond Ave Staten Island	at 9:30 a.m. on June 25th	Signed *Donald Olson* Pr.	
arrived at passed through New York City Hall ~~left~~	at 11:50 on June 25	Signed *John V. Lindsay*, Mayor	

The rest of the way across the Texas Panhandle went without incident. I managed 48 miles on the Tuesday, the biggest day's mileage since the second day of the trip, and the next day crossed the border into Oklahoma and reached the town of Sayre, doing 46 miles. The day's routine now had a firmly established pattern: four miles walking in the first hour of the day, five minutes to change from boots into my Adidas warm-ups and then just over an hour for another eight miles. This would bring me to about 10.30, and half an hour's blissful ease in the trailer, with Sue giving me iced coffee and cinnamon buns. Out again into the sun for another eleven or twelve miles before lunch—I would usually change into the lighter marathon shoes for this bit; it was a matter of striking a balance between the extra support given by the warm-ups and the faster speed which I could do in the marathon shoes. I was now running in four-mile stretches except when it got very hot. Every four miles Sue would be sitting in her car and she or Clive would hand me a drink and a cold sponge. If I was fresh, I would go straight on, but as the day went on the stops became a little longer, and I would sit on the edge of the car seat for a minute or so.

Being a compulsive timer, I would time each four-mile stretch, and try and get the twelve miles done in one-and-a-half hours. The sight of the caravan at the lunchtime stop gave me the kind of feeling that must manifest itself to the faithful getting their first glimpse of the towers of Mecca. I would put away several bottles of iced Schweppes, sitting at my ease on the long seat of the caravan, while Sue prepared lunch, and then revel in the pleasure of being able to eat as much as I felt like, and doze for an hour after it. When you are healthy and hungry, simple pleasures become bliss, I spent some happy moments dozing on that seat, watching the clouds drifting across endless blue skies until I too drifted into oblivion. I would wake up just before it was time to get started again, climb into my boots and roll off down the road before I was properly awake.

The other ingredient in my mental life which I have barely mentioned was the books I was reading. I took with me some poetry, *The Tin Drum*, and a book on psychology, all of which served to divert me from the monotony of putting one foot in front of the other for hour after hour. I was lent John Updike's *Couples*, which I couldn't manage to finish—I couldn't get in tune with the style, and eventually the cavortings of his sex-obsessed manne-quins ceased to interest me. I followed this with a paperback about drama in a great hospital, which was so incredibly trite that it vastly increased my appreciation of Updike's powers as a novelist. It was relief that I turned to *David Copperfield*; Dickens could never have sold his stuff if he had even touched on what was the main theme of Updike's book, but nevertheless his characters of 150 years ago were for me far more alive and real. Sue and Mark had both read the book earlier in the trip, so we could all discuss the characters and compare them with people we knew. Another book I read was Steinbeck's *Travels with Charley*, which of course had special interest for me.

So, between drinks, meals and books I managed to run out of Texas and enter Oklahoma. It was the end of a long hot day when I got to Sayre; as on leaving New Mexico I was forcibly struck by the difference between adjoining states, which one might think were separated only by arbitrary lines on the map. The towns we had come through in the Panhandle were most unremarkable—fungus growths sprouting out of the concrete, motels, stores, cafés and garages, each with its pin-head crop of signs jostling for attention, and few places in which one could imagine people actually living. In Oklahoma it was different—there were more hedges, more trees, and the towns had a recognisable centre, with two-storey brick buildings standing side by side, instead of the sprawl of bungalows.

We couldn't find a trailer park in Sayre, so stayed in the city park, a peaceful wooded place. One of the local police force came along to see us—more out of tedium than official zeal I think, and had quite a chat with us, showing Clive his gun. He came back later in the evening, looking for his dark glasses, which he had lost. The other visitor we had was the manageress of the park, a huge woman with dark eyes and a stern face. When we had completed the formalities and she learnt who we were she became friendly. She had an English friend—a most amusing woman, we really ought to meet her. She talked as if the English were a kind of pet, quite docile and guaranteed for a laugh. Later on, she brought two of her friends along to see us; one was very tall, about 6'3", and the other very square and solid, they came and peered at us as we sat outside eating curry; they stood side by side and communicating in high twangy voices.

That night the weather executed one of its astonishing volte-faces. The heat of the day had mellowed to a lovely evening, and I was sitting outside with Mark, smoking a cigar to keep the mosquitoes away, when we heard a storm warning on the radio. During the night it broke over us with horrifying force, as it had in the Salt River Canyon, it hammered on the roof, but the little caravan kept it all out. In the morning it was calm again, but the temperature had dropped 20°. It was perfect running weather, and what was more I had left Route 66 to go on to 152, a little used road which ran due east to Oklahoma City. It was dead straight but saved from monotony by the gently undulating hills. The scene might have been England, with white-faced Herefords grazing in the fields, little streams and clumps of trees, but while I was enjoying this my hip trouble started coming back, and I ceased to appreciate the country quite so much.

I had done a long first session of 14 miles when it came on again, and I could only manage eight miles more before lunch. Just before lunch, however, the scene was brightened by the appearance of a fellow-countryman, Donald McLachlan of the *Daily Mail*, who had come from New York to see me; it was a great luxury for us to talk to someone who could understand our comparisons, and share his views on the American way of life; while we were talking to him we were visited by some more friends, a young couple who had spoken to us on our way through Texas, they had seen us come through Phoenix, and passed us on their way back to Oklahoma, and now we were passing their home, so we felt like old friends, in comparison to our usual acquaintanceships of a couple of hours. It warmed up in the afternoon and running became easier again; we passed through Cordell in the afternoon—37 miles in a straight line from Sayre—and I ran another eight miles further before returning there for the night.

Friday was another day for my *Observer* piece, providing food for thought, rehearsing and polishing phrases that had come into my mind during the previous day. So much happened in every week; and it had to be boiled down to 700 words; I could put down the names of the towns and recount how many miles I had run, but it was very hard to communicate the experience, the continuous performance of the same routine against a changing backcloth, yet subtly different from that image, because the backcloth was a living one, and it could intrude upon and change the performance.

It was a beautiful day, not too hot, and after the rain everything was growing and blossoming. In England I can recognise and name most of the common wild flowers, but here they were strange to me; there were clumps of vetches in yellow and purple, deep red marigolds and elegant rose-like flowers with petals curved like crinolines. Amid all this sweet-smelling nature there was only one false note—the corpses on the roads.

I had become used to seeing squashed snakes and the occasional possum, but here the casualties were mainly tortoises. The tortoise, one might think, is a surly, introverted reptile, a hermit, and yet from the evidence I saw he must conceal wild romantic impulses behind his armoured shell. In spring he is seized with an urge to dash across the road and mate—every mile carried the bodies of those who had gallantly failed; but judging by the tortoise population of Oklahoma a lot more must have succeeded.

In addition to all this fertility, Oklahoma showed us another kind of richness—we passed several farms with natural gas tanks behind them, and here and there the 'Christmas trees' that mark the sealed-off top of an oil well. Sometimes there would be a pump, black and oily, working steadily in the corner of a field, continuous, uncomplaining. The villages were many miles apart; we were amused to see at one point on the road a little square wooden building, in a little square of pasture, with a notice 'Elk Creek Primitive Baptists'; in the right and left corners of the field were two minute white huts—presumably the primitive sanitation of the Primitive Baptists.

Towards the end of the day we came to the only town, Binger, whose only claim to fame was that it was the home of the catcher of the Cincinnati Reds, this fact was proclaimed on the sign bearing the town's name. Just outside Binger we were intercepted by the first of the TV crews from Oklahoma City. The interviewer jogged alongside me for a while, asking questions; I naturally slowed down for his benefit, and he managed to cover about half a mile, but he was clearly having trouble, as he had a good deal of weight to carry. Not to put too fine a point upon it, his belly flopped about as he ran, and I was rather horrified to learn that he was only a year older than myself. Here was a man of intelligence, well dressed, nice car, proud of his home, looked after his insurance and his investments, and yet he neglected his body completely.

For the third successive night we camped on our own. Maury had come out from Oklahoma City with mail for us and then gone back there; we weren't sure if it was pressure of work or the attractions of the big city. Anyway, it was just as well that he did. We found a very nice looking camp site beside a lake, but the gate was locked. Mark drove all over the place trying to find the owner, but he never turned up. The only resident was an Alsatian dog, who sat beside the gate, and he couldn't do much for us, so we settled down outside the gate, washed under the pump which was handily there and eventually settled down for the night. We were all thinking of getting to the City of Oklahoma the next day, so we weren't too fussy. Sue had run the last two miles of the day with me, as well as driving down to Anadarko to send off my *Observer* piece, so she was as tired as I was. During the night two car loads of young men drove up and stopped, apparently looking for a swim in the lake, but we laid low and said nothing, and they went away.

Saturday, May 24th, was a big day for us all. For one thing it was Clive's birthday, and that makes it a very big day, when you are seven years old. He was awake before seven, to see what presents he had got; there were two parcels from home, a game and a puzzle from Maury, a pen-knife and cowboy boots from us. Mark said he would have to wait for his, but when we got into town, he bought Clive a gorgeous tooled leather belt with a silver buckle, which was his pride and joy for the rest of the way.

Having got up early, I was on the road soon after eight, en route for the big city. Maury had warned us that we would have quite a big reception, so I wanted to get the miles done as soon as possible. As I approached Oklahoma City the road signs caused a bit of confusion. Having gone ten miles I came to a sign saying 'Oklahoma City 37 miles', and then two miles further on a sign saying 'Oklahoma City 29 miles', which agreed with my own estimate and was fortunately correct; it may be nothing to a motorist, but a few extra miles can be heart-breaking to a runner. As it was, I got 26 miles in before lunch, and was only 17 miles from the centre.

Our lunchtime stop was in a little suburb of the city—a pleasant village of bungalows, neat gardens and children. There was quite a little crowd gathered around the trailer; they were friendly but not at all pushing in their attentions. There were a couple of truck drivers who wanted to know how I did it, so I told them, and then I did another TV interview and had some lunch, while Clive held court outside with a number of other small boys. He was a bit upset to find that his horny toad, the one given him by Victor, had escaped in the crowd, but luckily there was a lot else happening that day, and he was quite philosophical about it. After lunch I jogged a couple of miles down the road to keep an appointment with the main body of newsmen.

We were introduced to one of the men I had been hoping to meet ever since the prospect of the run first became likely—the man who won the first transcontinental race in 1928, Andy Payne. He was about my height but stockily built, as many marathon runners are. His grey hair stuck out like a brush, and helped to give him even now a tough, combative look. Though it was over 41 years since his great feat, he was obviously well used to being treated as a celebrity and took the cameramen in his stride, as they took various poses of us together. It was comforting to meet this man, who had been till now just a figure in history, and to see him fit and happy; it was I suppose a kind of guarantee of personal survival.

Andy was very pleased to hear news of Pete Gavuzzi, who had played such a dramatic role in both the 1928 and 1929 races; we promised to pass on his good wishes to Gavuzzi when we got home.

The TV and press people kept us messing around for a lot longer than I really wanted, but the sponsors had to get their money's worth, and this was one of the most important places on the whole journey, so I couldn't really begrudge it. One good thing came out of it; all this ballyhoo was taking place on a vacant space in front of a bar, and the lady who ran the bar, gave me a six-pack of Coors beer in return for a photograph. I wondered, as I at last set off to run the remaining 15 miles, why it was that Oklahoma, in fact the West in general, contained so many strong women. Was it heredity or environment? I inclined towards the genetic explanation; assuming that the immigrant population contained women of sturdier than usual stuff, the pioneers setting out 100 years ago would have tended to select women who could pull their weight, handle a rifle and drive a wagon, rather than the purely decorative kind.

With the benefit of a good westerly breeze I ran briskly towards the distant towers of Oklahoma City, until they became obscured by the thickening growth of street lamps, poles and signs in the foreground. When I got into the city proper, I found that I had a police escort, which made things much easier. Two motorcycle cops preceded me. Sue and a police car followed behind; they took me straight across the red lights without having to check my stride; not having to hop on and off pavements, I could relax into a good 9 mph pace on the mainly downhill run. I had had some pain in my left calf during the morning, but this was now forgotten; with all this attention, the adrenalin was flowing through my system as it had not done since we left Los Angeles. I had, however, learnt to be more careful since then, and had two five-minute stops, once for drinks and once for ice cream. My escort took me around the west side of the centre, along tree-lined avenues and then on to the Expressway on the north side of town.

Oklahoma City has plenty of green grass, and it was looking its best for us. The police sergeant alongside me was very friendly, and keen to tell me what a fine city it was, and I certainly wasn't going to contradict him. As I was beginning to feel tired the end came in sight, and we finished the day in a style worthy of Hollywood, sweeping up to the doors of the new and elegant Ramada Inn with our escort, just after five o'clock in the afternoon. I had only done 43 miles, but it seemed good to stop there.

The rest of the day rightly belonged to Clive, who still had his birthday treat to come. He and Mark had gone on ahead to get in a swim during the afternoon, and after I had bathed and for a change put on some smart clothes, we all had dinner together in the motel. Clive's idea of the perfect meal at this time was fish and chips with tomato sauce, ice cream and Coke, and when he had his fill of that we all went to see *Oliver*. Nothing could have been better for taking all our minds off the rigours of the journey, and indeed away from America itself, than to sit, clean and well-fed, in our most comfortable seats and be carried into this world of colour, music and melodrama. It was a perfect ending and closed for me the second phase in my battle with the continent.

Chapter 8
Oklahoma City to Springfield, MO

It was Sunday morning, May 25th. For once I woke in a comfortable double bed, I had a shower and went over for breakfast; for Sue it was the utmost luxury not to have to prepare breakfast in the confined space of the caravan. I got on the road soon after breakfast, leaving the others to visit the Cowboy Hall of Fame. Being Sunday morning it was very quiet; the road running out of town to the north-east was a broad divided highway, with a wide strip of grass in the middle, so I ran on the grass, to ease the slight strain I felt in my left calf. I stayed on this for over an hour, passing the turnoffs to the turnpike, which I was not allowed to run on, and keeping on till I saw the signs for Route 66. This was now almost a deserted road, since the turnpike took most of the traffic, and it was therefore ideal for my purpose.

It was a dull, grey morning, in tune with the slight feeling of anti-climax that followed our bit of glory in Oklahoma. Just before break time I acquired some welcome company—Mike Lester, who worked for the *Tulsa Tribune* but was also the only registered long-distance runner in the state of Oklahoma. He did eight miles with me between break and lunch, during which time we reached what I then judged to be the halfway point, the village of Luther. Mike took a picture of me there, squinting into the sun, which is interesting in that it can be compared with pictures taken at the beginning and end of the run. It can be seen that although I had lost a lot of weight since I started, I did not lose any more in the second half. This agreed with my estimate of what would happen—that after a few weeks I would establish an equilibrium between my energy output and my food intake. At the time I started the run, Doctor Griffiths Pugh, our leading exercise physiologist, had cast doubts, in a letter to the *Sunday Times*, on my ability to take in enough calories to keep up with the expenditure; he had been flattering enough to say that if I succeeded it would be the physiological feat of the century. I certainly didn't agree with him about this, in the light of previous performances, but it made an excellent press story.

The weather was warming up again—I remember that Sue sunbathed at lunchtime. As we were on the quiet roads, all the others came out for a bit of exercise—Clive for his mile walk, Sue for a two-mile jog and Maury for a mile. Sue was with me when we reached the small town of Chandler, and as we came through the clock said 6.15 and the temperature read 83°. Mark took over for the last four miles, and I finished up covering 46.

It was curious in Oklahoma to see what a short history they had, more so because the country had such a prosperous and settled look. In the desert or prairie country, the effects of civilisation were merely scratches on a huge canvas, but here the pattern of roads and farms, cattle, hedges and telephone wires formed the landscape itself, and there was little to suggest that man had not been settled here for hundreds of years. The signs that this was only a recent occupation were quite small—in one place we saw a notice which read 'Do Not Shoot at the Telephone Wires'. It was a shock to us, who take anything built since 1800 as quite recent, to see an 1850 barn pointed out as an ancient monument, and to see the notices commemorating the start of the Oklahoma land run. 'On April 22nd, 1889,' the notice said, 'Oklahoma territory west of a line on which this notice stands was thrown open. At the firing of a gun, thousands of homesteaders started across the line to claim land for themselves, and two million acres were settled overnight.' It was a tremendous thing to contemplate, those thousands of men and women crowding out from the East to find room for their families to live, racing on foot and on horseback to find 160 acres of the best land they could.

There must have been some grim struggles, with each other and with the land, before today's farming pattern became established. One-hundred-and-sixty acres was barely enough to support a family in those days, and the farms now are much bigger. Only some of the soil will support arable crops; much of it is given over to grazing or to horse breeding, for which the State is renowned. One wonders what became of the people who could not support themselves and had to sell out; it was incredible to think that all this had happened in the lifetime of my grandparents, and even more incredible that it should be the people of this new country who were sending men to the moon.

Whenever I had a definite objective ahead the running was mentally easier; I could see the mileage shortening now to Tulsa, and although it was getting up towards 90° again, I had a successful day; I had decided now to make each of my four sessions twelve miles, now that I had no injury trouble, and try to get back on to my original schedule. The green country was in some ways harder to run through than the desert, its lushness seemed to speak of the easy life, the peaceful daily round.

This week seemed to be graduation time in a lot of high schools; often I would see the rows of chairs set out on the sports field, awaiting the moment when it would become for one sunny afternoon the centre of so much emotion and nostalgia. Once or twice I passed busloads of boys and girls on their way to the ceremony, the girls in white dresses with red ribbons, like something from Thornton Wilder, or like the pink and white flowers that blew beside the road. It is a basic human need to try and cut eternity down to a size that we can tolerate; it often gave me a strange feeling to think that I was briefly touching the lives of people whom I would never meet again, and so become an isolated speck on somebody's memory, forever frozen in that period of time. 'Do you remember graduation day, and how hot we got standing out on the field?' 'Yeah, and we saw that little guy who'd run from California, going right through town, all in yellow.'

Forty-eight miles that day brought me within two miles of Sapulpa, and I didn't feel bad; Mike Lester had done eight miles with me near the end of the day, and Sue did two miles as well. After supper we had an hour's daylight left, so I suggested to Mark that we walk the last two miles into town, to make it easier in the morning. Maury took us back to the right spot, and as we started our leisurely stroll we lit up the two cigars that I had brought along. We strolled towards the town, where the lights were beginning to show up against the deepening blue sky. I turned to Mark and said: 'Physiological feat of the century!'

We stayed that night in a motel, as there was no trailer park; it ranked as one of the most uncomfortable habitations I have slept in—the windows wouldn't open, so we had to have the air conditioning on, which was incredibly noisy and made the room too cold. Still, I never stayed awake long after a day's running, and slept soundly till it was time to get up and be on the road to Tulsa, just over 20 miles away.

Now that I was over half way, as well as getting further east, I seemed to be getting more publicity and more company, I think it may have something to do with the fact that having weathered the worst of the going, the chances of my succeeding were pretty high, whereas at the start I was just another nut trying to do the impossible. That day, for the only time, I had someone running with me all day. Before I had gone a mile in the morning, a college athlete called Bruce Martin turned up, and ran with me for the whole of the morning, some 23 miles. Four miles down the road, when I was about to change from my boots to my running shoes, a friendly chap from the Tulsa YMCA came along and presented me with a t-shirt; later he returned to jog along with me and record an interview on his tape machine.

I had been told before I started that jogging was very popular in the States, and though I wouldn't call it a mass movement, I did come across evidence of interest now and again. The most telling thing was that when I passed a gang of kids on the street, they would often shout out: 'there goes a jogger,' whereas in England they usually say: 'there goes a runner.' In both countries, of course, they shout out encouraging remarks like: 'One-two, one-two' or 'You're too late, it's gone', but I have learnt to ignore this. What I suspected, and what was confirmed by the athletes I spoke to, was that most children had never seen anyone running, except the odd 'jogger' taking a bit of gentle exercise, and even he was regarded as a bit of a freak.

In the afternoon I ran with a high school boy, and with Mike Lester for the last time. They all told the same story, that apart from school or college sport, there was no available competition for a runner in Oklahoma, and very little in the neighbouring states. I talked to them of running in Britain, of how I could get a race every Saturday of the year without travelling more than 50 miles; I talked about the excitement of the road relay races and the fantastic fields in the National Cross country championships; I talked about running in Europe, the fast tracks in the Scandinavian woods, the cross country races round football fields in Belgium, or round race-tracks in Spain; of the South of France, the dinners, the prizes, the chaos, the fun.

I have met a lot of American athletes, in the GB–USA matches and in the 'prestige' meetings around Europe, and very few have been able to regard their sport as fun; the few who can combine ability and dedication with a real love of life and their sport are the ones who become great. That is an overworked word, but it does describe men like John Pennel, Ralph Boston and Russ Rodgers, men whom I have met but a few times, but am proud to call my friends.

That was a full day. In the middle of the afternoon I had to put through a call to a radio programme in London. The only place available at that time of day was a roadside bar, so in I went. All the bars have darkened or shuttered windows, so that one can never see in from the outside, and inside is all cool gloom. A slim dark girl was playing pool with two men; when she spoke, she had a voice like a high-pitched buzz-saw. At the bar were a man and a woman, both middle aged, putting in a steady afternoon's drinking. The man was soft and pudgy, good-humoured; the woman was a small-town Bette Davis—she had that tragic gash of a mouth, poorly disguised with a lot of lipstick, and the piled-up hairdo one associates more with Rita Hayworth; she gave the deadpan performance which in films hides a maelstrom of tragedy, but I didn't have the time to get her story. For a few moments I was part of their world, then connected to a studio in London on a chilly damp night, and then I was back to my own reality again, straight road and 85°.

While I had been on the phone the entourage had increased by one more, a man called Jerry Hornig, who had cycled from San Francisco to New York in a record time seven years ago. He accompanied me for the rest of the day in his car, and on the last few miles I had Mike Lester and Mark running with me as well, so that it was almost a party. We found a trailer park in Claremore, and I went a few miles past it to get my quota in. As we had finished quite early, we had time to talk with the woman who owned it; her husband, who was a pipeline layer, was abroad somewhere, earning an enormous wage, and she was keeping this trailer park in Claremore, Oklahoma, between the Highway and the railway. She kept the place clean and changed the sheets. The swimming pool had a fence round it, a padlock, a set of rules (No running, No dogs, No drinks) and a sign saying, 'Swim at your own risk'.

After all that had happened that day, it was known as 'the day the trailer tipped up', because that was what happened, as we all sat down for supper together, Mark having forgotten to put down the supporting legs. Chicken fricassee was thrown everywhere, and bits of rice kept turning up in odd places for days afterwards.

All that night and for much of the next day we were serenaded by railway trains. Road and rail ran side by side here, and about every mile there was a grade crossing, with no barriers of any kind. Only a year before there had been a terrible accident, when a carload of children going to school had become stalled across the line; that awful day was now recalled by every train that passed.

Claremore was apparently dedicated to the memory of Will Rogers, the greatest figure that Oklahoma has yet produced, we had passed Rogers Street, the Rogers Museum and Will Rogers Airport, and now we were driving parallel to the Will Rogers Turnpike, this had the virtue of taking all the traffic, and effectively preserving the towns on the old road in an atmosphere of the 1940s. It looked as if nothing had been done in those towns since the turnpike had opened up and taken away most of their livelihood. The signs were lower, the paint was fading, children and dogs could wander across the street unmolested, and friends could hear each other talk without being deafened by the passing traffic. Places like Afton, where I finished the day's run, are a powerful argument in favour of decadence. Of course, places like that don't have trailer parks, but 14 miles ahead of us was marked the Twin Bridges recreation area, so we pushed on there, and found an excellent camp site beside the beautifully named Lake of the Cherokees.

We didn't see any Cherokees, but we did find electric points, showers and lavatories, and a place to swim and fish—all for a dollar. There were a good many other campers there, in tents, trailers and camper trucks, camp fires were burning, and more people came down to fish late in the evening; I had a delicious swim before dinner, and the next morning had a dip before breakfast, and another one in the middle of the morning, after I had run the 14 miles from Afton. Clive of course loved it, and Mark, who had always been a keen fisherman, stayed fishing with him the whole morning, getting one small fish, which they put back. As Maury had gone ahead to Springfield, Missouri, Sue alone came on with me, leaving the boys fishing at the camp.

After a few miles I crossed the Missouri border, on Route 60 now, as it was about ten miles shorter to Springfield that way than on Route 66. I stopped for a few moments to commemorate the occasion on celluloid, then continued my lonely way till lunchtime. That was five states crossed now, and each one about the length of England, though I was by no means taking the longest route across them. Over five weeks had gone, and not one had passed without showing us some novelty of the American scene. I could have travelled like this for 600 days without covering the same ground twice, and always found contrast.

This day, which had begun so peacefully, ended up with a lot of incident. In the afternoon I managed to detach myself from my supporting group, a rare achievement which I managed by taking Business Route 60 through

Neosho, whereas they thought I was staying on the normal Route 60, which bypassed the town. It was just coming up to teatime when I executed this rather subtle manoeuvre, and as a result had to run 14 miles instead of twelve in that session. While I was plodding through the town, Sue and Mark were brewing tea on the bypass, confidently expecting me to appear round the corner at any moment. When I didn't turn up, Sue suddenly remembered that I had muttered something about Business Route 60 earlier in the day. Being a girl of decisive actions, she just said, 'I know where he is,' and drove off. Mark drove off in pursuit without securing the caravan, so that when they caught up with me, having a drink of water in a milk bar, the floor of the caravan was awash with strawberry jam, oil and vinegar, water from the kettle and most of the pages of *David Copperfield*, whose binding had broken. We displayed our British phlegm by not losing our tempers with each other for very long—it was too hot for that anyway—and we went into the milk bar to drink delicious malts and cool down.

A 25¢ malt lies pretty heavy on the stomach, and I went slowly for a few miles after that stop, but I got moving again during the last five miles of the day. We went through the little town of Granby, an historic town almost 150 years old, and Sue did a couple of miles jogging with me.

When I reached the spot where 48 miles were completed for the day, and where for want of anything better we had decided to stop, I found a strange sight. The cars and caravan (with Maury, who had gone into Springfield) were pulled in to a field of long grass. On both sides of the road were clouds of white feathers. At this spot a truck had crashed the day before, killing the driver and releasing a vast number of White Wyandotte pullets, good layers, whose number was variously quoted as 4,000, 5,000 or 7,000. Though most had been recaptured, a good few hundred still crouched in the bushes, playing hide-and-seek with the local people, who clearly regarded roadside chickens as a gift from God. Several pick-up trucks were parked, and whole families with sacks at the ready were wriggling through the undergrowth, making encouraging noises in what we supposed to be the White Wyandotte tongue.

We took part in the game for a while, though there wasn't anything we could do with them when we caught them, and we got into conversation with some of the people. The most forthcoming was a man named Sam Allen.

Sam, we learned, was from Oregon. His father had been Irish and his mother Native American, which gave him a tribal name as well. He had blue dungarees, a checked shirt, and the kind of peaked cap that loggers wear. He didn't advise staying where we were; for one thing there were a lot of copperheads about (poisonous snakes) and for another, the company that owned the chickens would be back with a gang at nightfall, to recapture their property while it was roosting. Of course, this may have been a bit of Irish blarney designed to leave the coast clear for Sam Allen and his pals to collect some more free chicken dinners, but we weren't going to take a chance with the copperheads. If we went up the road a mile or so, he said, there was a new minister, be sure to give us some space. 'A stranger, he is, some kind of foreigner. Let me see, he's a Filipino, that's it. You go and see him, and tell him I sent you, if'n you kin' remember my cotton-pickin' name.'

I left it to Sue and Mark to work it out, put my boots on, and said I'd walk on down the road till they collected me. I got three miles in, bringing me up to 51, the longest day so far. Mark was waiting at a crossroads. They had been offered a place to park by one of the farmers, a friend of Sam Allen's who was also looking for his share of chickens. The car drove deeper into the country, and turned into a dirt road, sending up clouds of dust which hung behind us in the still evening air, long after we had passed. It was five miles to the farm, the furthest we had ever been off our route, and for once there were no trucks or trains to be heard. When I arrived Sue and Clive were firmly ensconced beside the farm house, Clive was being taken for a ride on the pony and shown all the puppies.

It gave us a glimpse of an America which I never dreamt still existed, the country life whose ways had hardly changed since the first settlers cleared the woods and put up a barn. The farmhouse stood in a small clearing, looking somehow hunched. Additions, outhouses and sheds nestled against it, and long grass ran up to the walls on two sides. Our host was a bearded man, in the universal check shirt and dungarees, with a white grin that would flash out from the surrounding darkness of his beard. He introduced us to his wife, a huge woman in a shapeless dress, a sort of archetypal 'Big Momma', with a wide range of children from her two marriages. There was a son in the Air Force, some girls who were playing with Clive, and some boys who were away at a barbecue and turned up later.

The animal life was even more productive, there was an Alsatian with a litter of puppies, a Tennessee coonhound—a beautiful black-and-tan bitch with silky ears—and two of less certain breed who fought, had to be chained up and barked all night. Over in the barn were a variety of fancy breeds of chickens, and two pedigree ducks, all scratching about on the earth floor. The whole effect was of people rooted to the earth, totally at odds with the fast-moving, safely-wrapped, drive-in and drive-out life that we had seen along the highway. There was no electric light, as the generator had broken down, so we turned in when it got dark, and watched the fireflies in the wood. We didn't have to waste any time washing, as they didn't have running water, and the lavatories were not so much of the pit type as the heap type, which didn't encourage one to linger.

When we came to leave in the morning, they were genuinely sorry to see us go, and gave us fresh vegetables from their garden. I suppose that they were the poorest people we met during our entire journey, and yet they gave us the most, because they gave of themselves, without affectation.

We took the road to Springfield, just over 50 miles away. It was my first full day in Missouri, and the difference in character from Oklahoma was marked. We were in the Ozarks, going through wooded hills. It seemed as if the settlers pushing westwards had missed this part of the country, and much of the original woodland still remained, though no doubt there was a good agricultural reason for this. It was interesting to run through, and one could easily imagine oneself back in the olden days, with Native Americans tracking through the woods and hostile eyes looking down from the bluffs.

Break time took me into the town of Monett, where it started to rain. Sue had a lot of shopping to do, and as I had to sign the traveller's cheque for her, I went into the supermarket with her. I followed her round, wearing of course my bright yellow running kit, while she trundled her trolley up and down the cornucopian alleys. When we stopped at the end of a row, I heard a rustling noise behind me, and looked round. Following us at about ten yards' distance was a little group of shoppers, stalking up under cover of their wire trolleys, while from the alleys we had passed heads craned out, at different levels. We were like people in a circus—a day in each town, strange people to be looked at, with funny accents.

It was still raining when I set out on the next stage, and I felt really at home, splashing through the puddles, cool rain on my face. The rest of the day contained minor incidents—a couple of high schoolboys ran two miles with me, a TV crew came out from Springfield, and I ticked off the miles at a steady pace. After tea, when Sue had gone on to the overnight stop, Maury and Mark looked after me, and it was while I was getting a drink from them that we witnessed a remarkable incident. We were on a straight piece of road, at the top of a gentle slope, when we heard an engine noise so fierce as to make us all look up. From the east came a big, low, car, an oldish model painted up, it was doing 80 or 90 as it came towards us, and as it came over the slight rise the driver was accelerating as hard as he could. Fifty yards past us there was a terrific bang, and bits of the car flew into the road, the back of it was scraping the ground as it continued down the road, slewing across to the left, where, thank God, there was nothing coming the other way, and then skidded into the dusty shoulder, coming to a halt on the earth bank.

We stood amazed for a second or two, and then Mark and Maury went down to see if they could help. I ran down the road in the other direction, and within a couple of hundred yards found a parked police car, which had been sent by the sheriff to keep a lookout for me. I told him about the accident, and he went off to investigate. Luckily no one was hurt; the two young men in the car seemed to take it all very lightly, and went off back to their other car. We had noticed that drivers in the States don't take the same care of their vehicles as the British do—they regard them as more expendable, but it was the first time we had seen anybody literally drive one into the ground.

The last few miles into Springfield were on divided highway, and slightly downhill; I completed 49 miles for the day (making 100 in two days), which put me less than ten miles from the centre of Springfield, and was then driven five miles on to our place of rest. That night we stayed in a mobile home park, one of the most pleasant we had seen, yet fairly typical of the conditions in which many mobile home dwellers live. When Steinbeck wrote his *Travels with Charley* he devoted a good deal of space to this modern phenomenon, so unlike the traditional view of what is the 'natural' way of life. He concluded that we have overestimated the importance of 'roots' as a basic human necessity. He may have been right in some ways—I would place freedom above roots in my list of the ingredients of happiness, but nevertheless, everybody needs to belong somewhere, and if you live in a mobile home park it must be that much harder to find out just where you belong.

Materially, the dwellers in this camp had a lot. Their homes were ranged in avenues, with wide grassy lanes between them and flowers and trees down the centre. The trailers were 60 feet long and ten or twelve feet wide; they were connected up for water, sewage and electricity; there were colour TV sets inside, awnings, garden chairs and children's playthings outside. In the centre of the park was a swimming pool; beside it a launderette—twin symbols of material well-being. There was no reason why a family should not live here for years, and some did, sending their children to nearby schools; at the same time it is quite straightforward to unscrew the connections, get a removal firm to put the home on a truck and take off for any place in the whole huge country that you take a fancy to.

These people are not burdened with gardens to keep up, lawns to mow or even houses to repair. If your home is getting a bit tatty, you can always trade it in for a newer model. So, we have a new species—Mobile Man. Perhaps it is an inevitable trend in social evolution. After all, it is only a very short time since the roaming tribes of hunters decided to build houses on poles in the centre of lakes or put up mud huts in the valleys of the Nile or the Euphrates. Now the tribes are at peace (most of the time) with each other, and they don't have to fear the wolves, the tigers or the bandits from the hills. Those who have the inclination can take up the wandering life and go where the pickings are best.

It seems quite plausible in the States, where roots in any case do not go very deep, but it doesn't hold up in Europe. Happiness to me means communities living together, giving and taking from generation to generation. I like to think that what I say and do matters to my friends, in the same way that their lives touch mine. The love and the experience, the unwritten skills of living happily together that my family has passed on to me, I would like to pass on to my children and my friends, so that when I die, I am remembered, not consciously, but because I am irremovably part of the lives of other people. You can't do that, living in a mobile home park, where the village elders are the TV newscasters, and the man next door is a stranger.

Chapter 9
Springfield to St. Louis, MO

We have now come 1,700 miles together, Dear Reader, but we still have a long way to go. It is over 200 miles to St. Louis, which itself is two-thirds of the way. If at times the day-by-day repetition of running and eating, sleeping and running, gets a bit tedious, think what it was like for me. We had experiences, great and small, which I am trying with the clumsy tool of language to get over to you, but these were spread thinly over the days, and most of it was just slog, slog, slog on the hard, dry road.

You will not understand the experience unless you can conceive of the feeling of moving with infinitesimal slowness over the huge tract of land lying between the two oceans. It will be a long time before we dip down to the sea. When you were a child, did you ever play hide and seek in the woods on a summer afternoon? The bracken seems a mile high; the flies buzz, ten minutes pushing through the undergrowth seems like an age; you are aware of every tiny moment of time passing. That was how it seemed to me—the slower you go, the more you see.

Now we are home and can digest the experience, I can see that things were happening at the same time on different levels of experience. The accumulation of days gave us the feeling of the country and the people, but each particular day was taken up, as days are, by trivialities, often commercial ones. As we relied on our sponsors to make the trip possible, we could not avoid giving them their money's worth in publicity. Once a week we rang a TV show in Los Angeles, and once a week the CBC in Toronto, which meant finding a phone booth and making a stop at the right time. On Wednesday and Thursday, I would start thinking about my *Observer* piece, to be written on the Friday. At any time of day someone might turn up, from a local newspaper or radio station, to ask questions.

We got through Springfield, Missouri, pretty smoothly on the morning of Saturday, the 31st. Mark had to go into the town centre to buy a replacement for the fountain pen he had lost. He always took great pains in writing letters to his various girlfriends, pinning the flimsy paper out on the table of the caravan to avoid it being blown about, and taking pride in his callig-raphy. While he was engaged in this important errand, I went around the edge of the city. In Europe you can tell when you are coming into a city, the size and age of the buildings increases, but here there is just a larger sprawl of one- or two-storey buildings, all of recent origin. There is a lack of local flavour, too; the same motels and supermarkets come up in every town—Safeway, A&P and even Piggly Wiggly stores; Howard Johnson, Quality Inn or Ramada Inn motels. We travelled on through Springfield, Missouri, without learning anything of the kind of people who live there, except that they appear to be like everybody else.

That morning we passed quite close to the 'Wonder Caverns' so Sue took Clive off to see them, after leaving the trailer parked twelve miles ahead of me. I was back on Route 66, major highway again, and pretty boring it was, too, luckily the mile marker posts reappeared, and I trotted out steady miles in under 7:30 apiece, and the slight uncertainty of making a rendezvous with the unattended caravan gave some interest to my progress.

I managed 24 miles both morning and afternoon, though the increas-ingly hilly nature of the country made the last session quite hard work. The road was now a switchback, with about a mile between each crest, as I topped one rise the vista of the next opened before me, while either side thick green woods, hid all but the roofs of the farmhouses. We found a convenient and uninhabited trailer park three miles short of my scheduled stopping place, in a pinewood, and Maury gallantly came out to run the last two miles into the camp. This time he managed half a mile with me, but I had to leave him then, and when I arrived in the camp, he was a distant speck on the horizon, a mile behind. Mark did the last three with me, giving me the chance to disguise the weary miles with conversation.

Sunday, June 1st, and we were a good bit nearer home. Now we could say we hoped to arrive 'on the 25th or the 26th', without having to add the name of the month. Now I could think of being home in a month, which with two months behind me seemed so much less than it had the day before. I seem to remember that I spent a lot of the day in calculation, firstly working out just how far I had to go to St. Louis, which was a variable quantity, depending on which map used, and then, having arrived at an approximate figure, calculating the total distance to New York in miles and days.

My original schedule called for me to arrive in St. Louis on Wednesday, June 4th, and as I was now only 170-odd miles from there, I was fairly certain of achieving that. I had been pushing for St. Louis for a week now, since leaving Oklahoma City, and getting in good mileages. I therefore decided to give myself as much rest as possible in St. Louis, and leave there on Thursday morning, on level terms with my schedule. On that basis I should be able to predict the likely date of my arrival in New York, approximately three weeks later, which my sponsors wanted to know.

I spent many hours in the evenings and during breaks, poring over my now rather dog-eared Rand McNally atlas and working out mileages back from New York. It was from this atlas that David McJannet had worked out the total distance back in England and taking the journey as far as St. Louis he was only ten miles short of the actual distance I had covered. My calculations made it 937 miles more to New York, and as I had done 330 miles in the past week, I decided to allow myself exactly 21 days for that distance. Although, it was tempting to aim for a flat 20 days, I decided in favour of discretion, which was a good thing, because the distance came out at nearer 960. Somewhere my mind had tired while adding up the miles from town to town, and jumped a stretch; or I had calculated miles from either side of a city and forgotten to add in the width of the city itself. Anyway, I nominated my arrival date as June 25th. The thing now was to get to St. Louis as early as possible on Wednesday.

The whole of that day went by without our stopping in a town or village; the few small places on the map were brushed aside by the great highway. The twin roads smoothed out the rolling hills into a succession of switchbacks, at times they split up, separated by 100 yards of scrubland or trees, swooping together again, where a concrete span and an off-ramp betrayed the presence of a village, then away side by side to the horizon. It was good weather for running, bright and sunny, but not much over 70°. Between my calculations I snatched at what crumbs of diversion there were—I read the billboards, already advertising motels in St. Louis, and the rival attractions of the Meramec and the Onondaga Caverns, which we had seen advertised back in Oklahoma. We were quite close to the caverns now, and hardly a mile passed without seeing a sign for one or another. As they usually put up the miles to each place, it gave me some slight feeling of making progress, which I find essential. I cannot conceive of undertaking a long solo ocean voyage, like that of the oarsman John Fairfax, who at the time I was running had been at sea four months. The monotony of the scene, the feeling of getting nowhere, would be too much for me, I am sure. The rolling hills of Missouri with their massed woods were rather like an ocean, but at least I could sit down if I felt like it. In the afternoon session I felt particularly bored and sleepy, and it was as much as I could do to go on running. I even missed the trains, which in past days we had often cursed as they rumbled past our trailer at night.

When I think back to the run in a random fashion it is often the trains that I remember, because they seem to epitomise the vastness of the American continent. On the plateau of New Mexico, you could see them miles away, a long snake of rattling trucks, carrying the materials of the country's wealth—cars to the West, fruit or timber to the East. They climbed up grades and wound through cuttings built by men long dead; as they passed, the names on the sides sang a song worthy of Walt Whitman. The great engines, as many as five pulling together, were from the Acheson, Topeka and Santa Fe, the trucks came from everywhere—there was the Frisco Line, the Wabash, the Rock Island, the Pennsylvania and Erie, the Hudson and Delaware, the Lackawanna, the Soo. They seemed to speak of an earlier America, when distances still meant risk and romance, the America of the navvies and the folk singers. The big grey motor trucks that thundered past me on Route 66 were doing the same job, and the men that drove them must have been just as tough, but the romance wasn't quite the same—can you imagine a guitar song about the Lee Way grocery trucks?

The day finished with a slow drag up a long hill, near St. Robert, I had done 48 miles again, but my left leg, which had had to do so much extra work during my injury period, was feeling rather strained. We stayed that night at Clintons Trailer Park, a friendly place, where Clive played with the Clintons' grandchildren. For days on end he had to behave like an adult, be quiet, be sensible, and spend hours in the car, but he seldom complained. It was only when he returned to his normal self, rushing about and shouting with other little boys, that we realised what an effort it must all be for him. He was seldom in bed before ten at night, because the caravan was our living-room as well as his bedroom, and at seven he had to be up with the rest of us, but he found a solution by sleeping in the passenger seat of the MGB most afternoons. Apart from preferring the open car to the Austin, Mark became rather a hero-figure to him, and they generally travelled together. It came to be a familiar sight to me, every time the caravan drove past, to see Mark's brown and bearded face over the wheel, and beside him Clive's blond head just showing over the top of the seat.

The next day at least brought incident, if not all welcome. I did the five miles into the trailer park before breakfast, and afterwards set out to walk for a bit, with Clive walking with me for two miles. Maury had gone ahead to St. Louis the day before, so when we arrived in Rolla at lunchtime there was a man from the radio station waiting for us. I remember that it was blowing very strongly, and every time someone came into the trailer the door practically blew off. At least we had managed to get off the highway into a car park, so were spared the blast of the trucks, which had been with us all morning. When I had answered the usual batch of questions, the radio man scuttled off with his tape recorder, and apparently put the stuff straight on to the air, because before I had finished my lunch, we had another visitor.

She came in uninvited and plunked herself down opposite us on the long seat on which I was intending to take my post-prandial nap. She wore the baggy Bermuda shorts and straight smock-type shirt that seems to be the summer uniform for middle-aged American ladies during the day, but when she spoke it was to reveal a Welsh accent so thick as to be almost guttural. It was lucky, she said, that she just happened to come in from putting out her washing, because she just heard the newscaster say that I was in Rolla, outside the garage. We heard that she had come from Swansea just after the war, that she liked it here, but wished that she could go home sometimes, that it was a long way. She wanted to know all the facts about our run, where we came from in England and what my job was. She devoured our replies like a vacuum cleaner, and with about the same amount of humour and sympathy, till at length I said that I really must get my rest, and she left. I hope somebody loved her, but I didn't.

By judicious walking I managed to prevent the pain in my left leg from increasing too much, but it became localised in my left calf and Achilles tendon, so I had to limit that day's mileage to 46, and even this was not completed till after seven o'clock. Sue went up to the Onondaga Caverns camp site, and Mark waited on the road to collect me, just past Cuba. Maury arrived, doubling back from St. Louis, and we set off in convoy, driving quite fast, as we had ten miles to go. The road took us well away from the main highway, along narrow roads. In Leasburg we nearly hit an old car meandering out into the middle of the road, and in the flurry, we missed Sue, who was waiting there by the telephone to put through my call to Canada. We therefore had the farcical sight of Mark and I dashing along towards the camp site to get back for supper, Maury trying to hang on to us, and Sue trying to overtake both of us. By the time she caught up and managed to make us stop, there was only ten minutes left before the programme we were ringing went off the air. Sue reversed madly, went into the ditch, roared out again, and took off with me back to Leasburg. I think that things must have been pretty quiet in Leasburg since the days of Daniel Boone, because when we roared back, they were only just dusting themselves off from our passage ten minutes before.

We got back to the camp site, not in the best of tempers with one another, and were not very sympathetic with the site manageress when she wanted another $1.50, because we had brought in an extra car. By this time, we had fixed ideas about what was a fair price to pay for a camp site, and she had fixed instructions to charge so much per car. The impasse was resolved by Mark driving the Austin away and parking it in the hedge half a mile off.

After these little troubles I enjoyed a shower, and having eaten a large supper, felt the sense of euphoria which comes at the end of a good day's exercise. This was partly due to the cool night, much cooler than anything we had experienced since leaving the mountains. It grew dark soon after supper, and the stars were incredibly clear. When we went to bed there was for once no noise of traffic, not even a distant train whistle, little country noises reached us from a long way off. Once in the night I had to get up and go outside; the stars seemed to be pressing down on the roof of the caravan and brushing the tops of the trees and the dark wall of hillside.

Night in the caravan always had a magic quality for me; I have always been happiest when close to nature, and every night I rested happily, close to the grass, between the fulfilment of one day and the promise of the next. We were then as much part of the country as a boat is part of the ocean, feeling its slightest movement. When we could get away from the road it was perfect, with the birds to wake us in the morning, instead of the thumping trucks.

On Tuesday morning I set off determined to get as close to St. Louis as possible. I had gone only a few miles when the pain in my left Achilles tendon became very sharp. I hobbled a mile or two to where the caravan was parked and rubbed some Elliman's on it. It was back to the boots for a few miles and with that and the half hour's rest it seemed to improve.

Before lunch I had to stop to put through a phone call to Los Angeles, which got cut off several times, losing me another fifteen minutes or so, still the urge to get on towards St. Louis was strong, and I cut down on my lunchtime rest to make up the time. The afternoon sessions had to be increased to two hours each—an hour's walking and an hour's running—which gave my leg enough rest to keep going, but the thought of going back to a crawling 40 miles a day was both worrying and depressing. I suspected that part of the trouble might be due to the fact that my running shoes were not giving me quite enough support—the marathon shoes, though light and comfortable, did not have much padding in, and my trusty warm-up shoes, which had done me so well, were becoming worn at toes and heels. Foreseeing this, I had wired the Adidas agent to send me a fresh supply and hoped that they would reach me in St. Louis.

In the afternoon we found a real treat for Clive—Jesse James Territory. This was a reconstructed period village, containing relics of the James Brothers, where a group of actors put on displays for the children. As Clive was the only child there, on a weekday afternoon, they put on a little sketch just for him, ending in the shooting of the Sheriff by Jesse. Clive was a bit taken aback by the realistic way in which he died and looked a bit worried as they carted the sheriff off to the undertakers, with his boots pointing to the sky, Sue sent him round to have a look, and he came back greatly relieved and reported: 'He's just lying there, grinning.' Later he had his picture taken with the James Brothers and the Sheriff, and the print which now hangs on the wall of his room at home is the envy of his friends.

I had fixed my sights that day on getting to Pacific, and when Sue and Clive got back from their outing they went on and found a trailer park. In the last session first Maury, then Sue, then Mark, ran with me, and in spite of the pain in my leg I reached my target, shuffling along with the stiff, 'old man' gait that put the least strain on my tendons. It wasn't much of a place, close to the road, behind a garage, with no shower, but it meant that I could get a prompt start in the morning. St. Louis had come to be a major landmark to me—two-thirds of the distance gone, the Mississippi River to cross, and, best of all, half a day's rest, more than I had had in the whole trip. I was only 26 miles from the motel which Maury had booked for us, so reckoned to get there by one o'clock. I thought of having a swim in a pool in the afternoon, instead of pounding the road, dressing for dinner in a leisurely manner, and after a meal and a cigar we might take in a bit of good jazz.

The next morning, I was up at seven, and got out on the road for five miles before breakfast. Sue took the caravan out of the grimy car park and on down the road; when I came upon them, they were parked in a quiet bit of frontage road, separated from the highway by a broad slope of grass. The morning sun was slanting through the trees, warming the stiffness out of my leg. When I reached the caravan, my grapefruit was on the table and the bacon sizzling in the pan. After breakfast we had a visitor—Michael Cook, of British Leyland Motors, who had come out from New York to get some pictures of the cars and see how we were getting on. He took pictures all along the run, which provided a welcome distraction, and it didn't seem long before I had covered another twelve miles and could relax again. This bit of highway runs into the city through woodland; there seemed to be fewer billboards about, and the impression was a pleasant one, besides this, it was mostly downhill.

After my break I walked for a few miles, to give my leg a bit of rest, and then put my running shoes on again for the last stage into the city. Route 66, on which I had travelled so many miles, split up in a maze of flyovers and crossings, and I found myself on a city street, with a heavy stream of traffic in both directions. It was about this time that my reception started to build up. I already had our two cars and the trailer, Maury in his camper and Mike Cook in another Austin America, we were joined first by an agency photographer, then by a TV cameraman, then by a journalist and a photographer from St. Louis. As each had his own car, we were beginning to cause a bit of a traffic hazard. The road was too narrow anyway to handle the traffic, and there was no sidewalk. I had to stop and walk for about a mile, to let the reporter get his story, and let the photographer get some pictures of him running alongside me.

It was during this time that I got closer to being run over than at any time on the trip. I was walking along the right side of the road, something I would not normally do in traffic, and because I was talking to the reporter, I wasn't concentrating on keeping out of the way. The cars coming from behind me were streaming past two abreast, and one of them came so close that it clipped my hand as it swung by my side. It didn't hurt me, but three inches closer and the run would have ended there. For the rest of the trip I never let my concentration slip when running in traffic, and I always ran on the left, where I could see what was coming towards me.

I got to our motel just after one o'clock, but it was some time before I got the rest I was looking forward to—there were two TV crews waiting to do an interview, two news photographers and a man from the *St. Louis Post-Dispatch*. It was after two before I could sit down to lunch, during which the third TV station arrived, but having had a short day, and being delighted at being in St. Louis, half a day in front of my schedule, it didn't worry me at all. We had a big bunch of letters from home, and my shoes had arrived from Adidas.

After lunch I had a hot shower, lay down, and considered my surroundings. The motel had been picked because it lay on my route, on the west side of the city, and was comfortable. It was a remarkably pure and untouched example of the 1930s architectural style that I would describe as Egyptian Hollywood; the combined cabins and garages were built of yellow brick, with rounded corners, which contained those translucent glass bricks so typical of the period; both the windows and doors were topped by broad curved arches, and the fittings were of chrome. Though I am sure it will never happen, that motel ought to be preserved as an architectural and social monument to the Thirties. I say 'social' because this particular motel still had a reputation for 'naughtiness', which at one time was inseparable from the motel image. It occurs to me now that the reason why this place continued to be outstanding in this respect was the fact that the garages were integral with the rooms, and it was possible to drive into the garage and walk through a connecting door into the bedroom. Whatever the reason, all the newsmen had a good laugh when they heard where we were staying. 'You won't get much sleep there,' they said. 'It's all coming and going. Are you booked by the day or by the hour?' Like most reputations, it was exaggerated, and we had a most comfortable stay.

My half day's holiday did not quite live up to my hopes. For one thing it clouded over in the afternoon and it was not hot enough for a swim. Then the evening meal fell a little short of the standard I had expected in a major city. The experience was one which became depressingly familiar when we ate out. I suppose that we differed from the majority of clients in sitting down hungry at the table. It was never less than 30 minutes to get some food inside us, and this was usually the salad, the other starters being an unimaginative soup or a bit of frozen prawn. The main course suffered equally from the effects of the freezer, which took all the flavour out of the seafood. As a change from the ubiquitous steak I tried some veal scaloppini Marsala, but the meat was not tender, and the sauce was crude. The wine was cold and dull on the palate, and I had to console myself with the ice cream sundae and the coffee, which was at least of reliable standard. It was a meal, we were no longer hungry, but that was all you could say about it. As it was just as good as most of the meals we ate in the West and Middle West, one assumes that most Americans are satisfied with that kind of food, for a cost of £2–3 a head, a price for which I would expect a meal of character in Europe. Part of the trouble lies in the difficulty in creating a satisfactory ambience in which both staff and guests can feel at home—the only ideas of creating atmosphere in the West seemed to be dim red lighting and large menus.

We never got to listen to any jazz in St. Louis. We drove downtown and tried all the places that had been suggested to us, but there seemed to be nothing on, on a Wednesday night, so I never got my St. Louis Blues. We found a bar where there had been jazz earlier in the evening, we found a beer hall where they had banjo music, but they wouldn't let us in without our ID passes; we finished up by driving to the foot of the Gateway Arch and looking out over the river.

No minor disappointments could have spoilt that evening for me; it was enough to be there. For the first time in weeks I felt able to step back from the obsession of the run and look at the whole scene in a detached manner. Mark, Sue and I were sitting in our MGB, on a warm night beside the Mississippi; if I tipped my head back, I could see the smoke of my cigar dispersing the light of the mercury lamps; above that was the magnificent curve of the great Arch, its burnished steel plates catching the lights, its crest soaring to a height that made your head reel. If I looked out in front of me, I could see the wide river lowing quietly on its way to the Gulf; outlined by lights against the blackness were the riverboats, once potent symbols, now resting like old carthorses out to graze. Behind me were the new buildings, now rising from the grubby remains of the nineteenth century; the Busch Stadium gleamed with light, a modern Colosseum, with every one of its tiers of arches shadowed by the floods. Behind that I knew were the numbered rows of empty streets and avenues, each gloomy facade masking the lives of hundreds of Americans; in the corner bars languid girls talked on low limpid voices, and men with world-weary faces stared at them over their whisky. Beyond the streets were the vacant avenues of the suburbs, stores with deserted car parks and neon signs repeating their trite messages endlessly, with nobody to watch. Beyond that was the open country, forests and farms and deserts stretching 2,000 miles to the west, where the breakers of the Pacific still fell on the coast that I had left six weeks before.

Unlike Los Angeles or New York, I had no preconceived idea of St. Louis, yet the name itself was a symbol of America, the America of the songs, and it is the songs more than anything else, more than even Hollywood, that have created the image of America in older civilisations. Perhaps the name was emotive because it had meant so much to the pioneers, a symbol of security, city life, sophistication even. This is the key to it; this is what has given magic to what appears to a European to be a tawdry and transient city.

When you consider that in 1805 it took Lewis and Clark over two years to travel from St. Louis to the West Coast and back, when you consider that 100 years ago the West was merely scratched by a handful of trails, and when you consider that there are now great cities where two generations ago there was only a huddle of tents, then the magnitude of the American achievement comes home to you. The energy and the material wealth are amazing in themselves but in St. Louis, for the first time, I noticed something more—the first signs of the elegance and civilisation which is growing on these foundations, and which will within another generation equal anything we have in Europe. It could be seen in the new buildings, and in one or two of the suburban stores, though the texture of the meat and the temperature of the wine at the moment fall far below the standards of Chelsea or Montmartre, it does not do to sneer, because in 20 years, or even ten years, it will be all right.

Chapter 10
St. Louis to Indianapolis, IN

I left St. Louis on the morning of Thursday, July 5th. My few hours of peace were at an end, and, as if to make up for it, we had more than our usual share of the PR side of things. It started in a leisurely enough fashion; I was able to lie in bed till nearly eight, and then saunter over to the restaurant opposite for a plateful of hot pancakes and maple syrup. I had my new warm-ups to run in, and they made all the difference to my running, taking the strain off my sore tendon completely. I had to run down the road about a mile, before rendezvousing with the Schweppes people and the police escort that was going to take us through town. There we had a certain amount of picture-taking, and I set off to run a further nine miles down to the river.

The manager of the local Schweppes bottlers, Bill King, was a keen jogger and had been a miler in his high school days, he accompanied me on this stretch, which made a welcome change. He started off with the intention of running a couple of miles but got quite carried away by the occasion and in spite of increasing blisters kept with me all the way down to the bridge, which for a man of 40 was good going. We trotted through the streets, stopping for traffic lights, the towering Gateway Arch came gradually nearer across the rooftops, a few people came out of their shops to see us pass by, and one or two gave me a clap, it was tempting to speed up a bit from our jog-trot, but I knew from experience the dangers of doing that early in the day, particularly in traffic. My tendon didn't bother me at all, and everything went well for about an hour.

The plan as I understood it was to run down to the Arch and rest there for a bit, while a photographer took some more pictures of the car and caravan; however, as we approached the river, I noticed that we were on a road running parallel to the river front, so that we came slowly abreast of the Arch. When eventually we turned right, heading due east, towards the river, I could see that we were aiming directly for the Eades Bridge, which was upstream of the Arch. I asked Bill King if we were going to the Arch, and he asked the motorcycle policeman who was leading us. He said he had been told to take us over the Eades Bridge, and knew nothing about the Arch. As I knew Maury had booked a photographer, I swung away from the bridge and went down a slope to a car park, quarter of a mile north of the Arch.

It took some time for all our accompanying vehicles to get themselves parked, and then there was a consultation which resulted in all the vehicles being driven round the Arch, and brought right up to it, on the bumpy track that we had used the night before. This had the result of bringing out the attendants who control access to the Arch, saying that we weren't allowed to be there. I took a bottle of drink and lay down on the grass some way off, I could see the groups arguing, the police, the attendants, the Schweppes men and the British Leyland men. The photographer who had been booked had gone away to another job, so eventually someone borrowed my camera and took some pictures.

It was after eleven o'clock when I got under way again. The Eades Bridge over the Mississippi is long but not especially grand; it has toll booths at the east side, which charge a quarter for cars, but nothing for runners. When we reached the other side our police escort said goodbye and turned back into Missouri. We were now in East St. Louis, in the state of Illinois, and a more depressing collection of streets I never saw. It hadn't got enough of a centre to be called a town or a city, and yet it housed thousands of people. The paint was shabby, there were few advertisements, grass grew between the paving stones. It had the drab and unloved air which reminded me of Eastern Europe. There were so few directional signs that I had to ask the way in a gas station—most traffic, of course, goes straight out on the freeway, Interstate 40, so never sees this part.

I ran through streets of run-down houses from the last century. Slim, stylishly dressed young men wearing sharp hats and rings on their fingers lounged on the steps, smoking. As I passed one would say something and the others would laugh. I passed a high shabby brick building, iron-fenced, and was amazed to see that it was the University of Southern Illinois, previously known to me only by the athletes it had produced. I was not sorry to leave the inner city and get out into the greenery of the suburbs. East St. Louis worried me not so much because of the obvious poverty but because it had the feel of a defeated city.

Each state had its own atmosphere, and in Illinois it was that of a flat land lying under the sun. There were fewer trees and hills than in Missouri, more dust, heat and humidity. Eleven miles east from the Mississippi had brought me to Collinsville, a long straggling suburban town. I was still on Business Route 40, rather than the through highway, so this was a homely place, catering for its own needs rather than the passing traveller, and therefore generating more sense of being a community. It was very hot and close. Even after my lunch and rest—in the car park of a Piggly Wiggly supermarket—I didn't feel really refreshed; the excitements and interruptions of the morning, as well as the previous night out, had left me a bit jaded.

I walked for the first four miles in my boots, and as it was so hot, I discarded my t-shirt, I then found that instead of having gone through the town centre as I thought, I had to go along about half a mile of busy street. I felt more than usually self-conscious, clumping through, past the shops, wearing nothing but my bright yellow shorts and my brown boots, which seemed enormous on the end of my skinny legs. When I changed back into my running shoes, the prospect of running another 20 miles that day seemed appalling, but as happened often, I got a lift at just the right moment.

I turned out on to the main road, Interstate 70, and sitting on the fence of the frontage road was a boy in running clothes and a little woolly cap. He and some of his friends from the high school had been waiting for me since midday. He ran with me for a couple of miles, where we met two other members of the team, who had been brought along by their coach. It was heartening to meet with this enthusiasm, in a place where the climate was so much against running long distances, and I was able to forget how hot I felt, in talking about athletics, finding out what they had done and what they hoped to do. Their coach, a young teacher, was obviously a man of inspirational ability, he was doing what happens over and over again, bringing something new into the lives of these young-sters, and by helping them to overcome the difficulties of training and racing, helping them to master themselves. Between them they kept me going until teatime; we were parked beside a graveyard, talking about running, when a cop came, but instead of moving us on he told us that he was a jogger too, and wanted to know where he could get some good road running shoes like mine.

Six miles more, mostly on the frontage road bordering Route 70, all flat, and we came to Highland, where Maury got a motel room and we parked the caravan outside his door. I had a cold shower there, and set off with Mark, to do another four or five miles before the end of the day. It was already six o'clock and I was tired, but we managed another six miles before Maury collected us off the road about ten to seven. Even after a cold shower my body temperature felt very high, and it was a long time that evening before I was cool enough to sleep soundly.

Friday was a good day, with the minimum of interruptions. I was on the road at 8.15, and did 14 miles in under two hours—after yesterday's experience I wanted to get plenty of miles in before it got too hot. We found that what had been marked on our map as 'projected freeway' was already reality. This was another thing that impressed us: the way in which the freeways were pushed through; in Britain it has taken ten years for the M4 to get as far as Maidenhead, 30 miles out of London, and goodness knows how long it will be before the next 20 miles is built. The difference is that the land in the Thames valley has been lived on since the Romans did their bit of agricultural colonisation 2,000 years ago, and there is rather more preoccupation with the rights of the individual.

Anyway, Route 70 went arrow-like to the east, leaving narrow, placid Route 40 to the farmers and to us. The first few miles took me into Pocahontas, where trim white-painted wooden houses stood on green lawns; you never see the hedges, fences and walls that divide up English villages into a group of little fortresses. The road was worn in places, so that you could see underneath that it was made of bricks placed on their sides, with tar over the top, a construction I had never seen before. The road was so quiet, and the sides so overgrown that the birds hopped about unafraid, and once I saw what I think was a woodchuck staring indignantly at me from the verge, as if I had just woken him up. The road crossed to the north side of the freeway and then ran alongside it. We took our break beside a bridge which crossed it, and after this Maury left for Terre Haute and Indianapolis, taking with him my *Observer* piece for dispatch. After break the temperature was creeping up towards 90° but this troubled me less than the day before. I stopped for a few minutes to talk to a man from the Greenville paper, who wanted to know the story of my life, then went on to do twelve miles before lunch.

Every few miles along the road towns or villages were marked, but as the atlas showed the same size dot for populations from 0 to 1,000, we never knew quite what to expect. Sometimes we would find a little town with a store, launderette and the other essentials of life, sometimes just a road junction and a farm house. After a pleasant lunch stop in a shady lane Sue and Clive went off to Vandalia, to do the washing, and I followed. Vandalia turned out to be a large and bustling place, with an historic old State House where Abraham Lincoln had sat in the legislature. When I got to the centre I saw a man in a radio van, who started to come over to me; I kept on running and went away from him, so he jumped into his van and pursued me; he did an interview holding the microphone out of the side of the van, until I came to a garage where Mark had stopped to give me a drink. He talked to Mark for a bit—Mark's first experience of being interviewed live, which he handled very easily—while I consumed a lot of drink and a salt tablet. I learned that it was 95°, which accounted for my thirst.

I still had four more miles to go before tea, normally just a matter of routine, but this time it suddenly got very hard, the sweat was pouring off me, and I felt a bit sick, but I took it steadily, and was soon in the shade of the caravan, enjoying an iced drink. It was at times like this that I marvelled again at Don Shepherd's feat—how on earth did he manage when it got really hot, going sometimes for ten or 20 miles between towns? I suppose that one adjusts to whatever situation one is in, but it must have been very tough at times. I gave myself nearly an hour's rest, instead of the usual half an hour, and when I set off again the heat had gone out of the sun it was down to about 85. I went on to complete 48 miles for the day, finishing five miles west of Altamont, where Sue had found a first-class camp-ground.

There was a large grassy field with electric hook-ups, a lake to swim or fish in, and even a pitch-and-putt golf course. The owner of the site made us feel very welcome, and we all relaxed and enjoyed ourselves. Being a Friday night, the camp ground was filling up rapidly, and Clive, who had gone off to play on the swings, was soon the centre of a big bunch of children. We all swam—absolute bliss after a day in the sun—and ate our dinner outside in the cool of the evening. After dinner Sue and Mark went on the pitch-and-putt course, while I followed slowly. The greens were made of AstroTurf, the synthetic grass which had recently come into use on some of the indoor stadia. It had little to recommend it as a putting surface as it was too rough, but one could see that for games with a larger ball it could have slot advantages over the home-grown stuff.

Being one of the first arrivals on the camp site gave us plenty of chances to observe our neighbours. There seems to be a fallacy about that Americans are completely subservient to the car and the television, but we saw plenty of evidence of the boom in the outdoor life. Both tents and caravans were bigger and more comfortable than the average one sees on a European site, but this is the result of having more money to spend. The things that impressed us most were the trailers and the campers; in the States the term 'trailer' covers what we would call caravans, but I am referring to the trailers which could unfold to form the base for a tent.

The trailers themselves take up little space, but the dwelling which finally emerges is of real family size. The camper trucks were a familiar sight to us yet are hardly ever seen in Britain. They consist of a caravan-type body mounted on to a pick-up, usually with a section protruding over the top of the cab, which houses an extra bunk. A lot of families seemed to have a pick-up as their second or third car, and then buy a camper body to go on their holidays; sometimes we would see the body mounted on bricks in the garden, like a marooned boat. We saw so many of these on the road; they make an ideal holiday vehicle, but they just don't exist in England—I suppose we can't afford them.

Back on the road next morning, Sue and I were on our own, we left Clive and Mark fishing in the lake, and Maury was still in Indianapolis. I made 26 miles in the morning, reaching a little place called Montrose, very quiet, where we parked under a tree. We talked to an old man at a filling station—another place passed over by the highway, dying slowly, but a good place to retire to.

In the afternoon things became much less restful as the freeway died out, and all the traffic was on the same road as me, there was no hard shoulder for me to run on, so that every few yards I had to hop on to the rough grass or stony verge, to avoid the streams of cars and trucks. Our teatime stop was on the verge, at a point where the trucks were going flat out at the bottom of a slope, and we had to endure the continuous blasts of sound and hot air as they came past us. It was with the utmost reluctance that I got out again, with 38 miles behind me, to run the last ten or eleven miles into Casey. I hated the road, I hated the trucks and their drivers, I hated the sun and the dust. I found that this mood often came on me in the last session, and it was partly due to the fact that Sue and Mark would always leave me at this time to go and find a camp site, so that I never knew exactly when they would be coming back. Logically there was no reason why I should not run six or seven miles on my own, just after having had a rest, but yet the mood of despair would always get me at this time, once I had only four or five miles left to the end I cheered up, which proves something, I suppose.

On this occasion I was plodding along in my disgruntled mood when I saw a white MGB approaching, I assumed it was the others coming back, but as it got closer, I saw it didn't have our yellow signs on it. Nevertheless, it slowed down, and the driver put his head out of the window. It was my friend Alan Launder, formerly a fellow teacher in England and now a lecturer at the University of Western Kentucky. I had been half expecting him to turn up, as we were only 200 miles north of Bowling Green, and he was the kind of man that doesn't let his friends down. Term had ended the day before; Alan had driven the 200 miles with his wife and two small children and had calculated where I was likely to be on that day. A few minutes later Sue turned up, and they all went off to the camp site in Casey together, leaving me to run in, in a much more cheerful mood.

That Saturday night was one of our best. Sue had not been able to find a trailer park, and as Maury hadn't got back from Indianapolis, we didn't need a motel, so had been recommended to the Casey City Park. We parked there, for nothing, there was an electric hook-up, lavatories and wash basins—all we needed—and there was a first-class swimming pool, where we took the children. Now Casey is a little town of 3,000 people, not very different from hundreds of others, and that park catered for every possible form of recreation. There was a baseball field, with a Little League game going on with great enthusiasm, swings, a lake, a shooting range and a little stadium. This was the scene of great activity, as there was a dirt-track car race in progress. The course was a simple loop around straw bales, and the drivers were being timed over three laps, as qualifying heats for the race later on.

It was a colourful scene, with the drivers in tight overalls in the same racing colours as their cars, carrying the names of their sponsors, and a noisy one too, as the high-pitched engines warmed up in the pits, and the crowd yelled their encouragement. What impressed us most of all, though, was the demeanour of the drivers, who were between eleven and 14 years old. It was a Kiddicart meeting, with I suppose three or four dozen entries, each with their complete uniform, tight overalls, crash helmets and skin-tight black leather gloves, which they smoothed on linger by finger as they waited impassively for their turn. The cars, only four feet long, were beautifully turned out and tuned; the whole thing was in deadly earnest, and the mums, dads and big brothers yelled with an enthusiasm which at times caused visible embarrassment to the subject. I may appear to harp on the subject, but this was just one more example of material wealth—those cars would cost $200 or $300 each, and the uniforms a good bit too, and there were 40 of them in this little park in a small town in the rural part of Illinois.

How long time seems to stretch when you can recall every minute of it. As darkness fell in the park at Casey, the insects came out, millions of them, and we had to eat inside the caravan with the door closed. After dinner we talked for hours before going to bed, and even then, we had to spend half an hour killing the majority of the crawling, hopping and flying things which had found their way in. Sunday morning came, and the insects vanished with the night. Alan had to be back in Kentucky the next day, but decided to go with me for one day, and travel back at night. We sent the wives and children off to the Lincoln Trail State Park, 20 miles ahead, while Alan looked after me for the morning. For the first five miles I ran on an old road from Casey to Martinsville, but from then on, I was on the major highway again, dodging the traffic.

During my morning stop we had a good talk about our views of Britain and the United States. Alan felt that we were slipping behind in Britain because of our unwillingness to exploit our talents to the full, and in particular because of the lack of drive in our educational programme. In the States, 80% of the children stay in school till 18, and about 33% go to college. The figure in England for University or the equivalent is more like 10%, and the majority of our kids still finish their education at fifteen. In the States, as I saw for myself, there is a hunger for education, people are prepared to go back to school and retrain for new jobs, fathers expect their children to get a better education than they did, and they are prepared to go to a lot of trouble and expense to make sure that their town has a good school. In England we are still training an elite and neglecting the majority of our population. I reflected on Alan's words as I continued on my way, and they made sense. It would cost a hell of a lot to give every child in the country a good education up to the age of 18, but if we could afford it, it would completely change the nature of our society.

When I had completed my morning stint of 24 miles Alan drove me down to the Lincoln Trail Park. Another example of American wealth and planning. It was a huge wooded area, hundreds of acres, with camping and picnic places concealed in the groves. Picnic tables, lavatories and showers were tastefully laid out, roads had been built, but 90% of the area was natural woodland and lakes, with enough facilities for people to enjoy their leisure without discomfort. Once again, this is planning for the majority, rather than for the hardy minority who prefer to live rough in complete seclusion. Mark fished, the children played in the woods and the rest of us sunbathed and talked. I had to get on the road, but this time I had something as a goal—getting across the state line into Indiana and passing through Terre Haute. It was one of those days when every point seems to be a mile further on the map than on the ground, but eventually I picked my way through the new highway construction work and ran down the main road into Terre Haute.

Three miles outside the city I picked up a running companion, a genuine marathon runner, a native of Terre Haute called Joe. Joe was a dedicated runner of a type more often met in England than in America; he trained steadily and competed whenever he could, which in Indiana was very seldom, running was his main interest in life, and it was hard to find out much about the other sides of his existence. He had run the Boston marathon that year (it took place on April 21st, the day that I left Los Angeles), but had not done much since, as he had promised his wife he would redecorate the house. In spite of this, he ran with me for the rest of the afternoon, covering 17 miles, for which I was most grateful.

In Terre Haute we had a police motorcycle escort, and quite a bit of attention from two TV crews and various press photographers. The weather turned cool and cloudy, as we crossed the long iron bridge over the Wabash River, going into the town, I could see heavy rain clouds gathering. Being a Sunday afternoon, the city was deserted, but there was little of architectural interest to see. There was a legislature building, built in solid nineteenth-century Civic Baroque; the city showed a trend to a more European style of construction, which we noticed as we got further East—the buildings tended to be taller and closer together than those in the more spacious West.

In crossing the State Line, we entered another Time Zone, and came on to Eastern Standard Time, the same as New York—an encouraging thought.

This meant that our tea break that day came at six o'clock instead of five o'clock, and my last session didn't start till about quarter to seven. We were lucky in that the rain didn't start until the moment we stopped for tea, but when it did everyone crowded into the caravan—the four of us, Maury, Alan and Jenny Launder, their two children and Joe. When it eased off, and we started running, Joe asked me if it was like that all the time; I said no. Everyone was talking and eating, and in the middle of it the youngest Launder had pulled Mark's cup of hot tea all over himself, resulting in screams and chaos. It was quite a relief to start running again.

I had hoped to get as far as Brazil that night, but it turned out to be nearer 51 miles from Casey than the 49 shown in the atlas, so when we reached the trailer park after 47 miles I decided to quit there. It was 8.15 local time, and Joe's legs were feeling the strain. He rang his wife to tell her where he was, and I went off for a shower. The place we had found was another mobile home park, but not so spacious and well-appointed as the one near Springfield. The shower facilities were rather primitive, and there were little notices stuck up around the place. Beside the rather dubious cistern was a notice saying, 'Put Your Trust in The Lord', and in the women's loo was another saying: 'No drinking. No wild parties, or else OUT.'

I noticed that throughout the evening we were being observed by an old man in the caretaker's cottage, who sat in his rocking chair and stared at us through the window. It was while we were sorting ourselves out there, and the Launders were preparing to drive home, that we found that we had left the electric lead for the outside hook-up back in Casey. Sue and Mark went back for it that night, but without luck; we had had a lot of trouble getting a plug for it in the first place, and as we only had two weeks left, we decided to rely on gas power the rest of the way.

On the Monday morning, June 9th, I started my eighth week of continuous running, though of course the 49th day was not officially completed until 2 pm, because of the time change. I had made a new schedule for the rest of the way, aimed at reaching New York on the 25th; unlike the original, this had no allowance for rest days, though the last day in each of the remaining three weeks was slightly shorter than the others. This meant that I had to be at a certain place on the ground at the end of each day, instead of merely keeping to a daily average, as before. The main psychological effect of this was that I worried about the accuracy of my maps, and spent most of my breaks poring over them, I had the Rand McNally atlas, the Triptik made out for me by the Automobile Association of America, and the state maps which we were given at the filling stations; it was rarely that all three agreed about the distance to the next stop, so I used to take a majority opinion.

It was during that day that I discovered that I had forgotten about Indianapolis! I had calculated the mileages from either side of it and omitted the eleven miles from one edge to the other. There is nothing more annoying than a mistake you make yourself, because you can't shift the blame, and I was in a bad humour for several miles. I got around the problem by running 48 on the last day of the week instead of 40 and putting an extra mile on to the other days. Apart from this mistake the day was not unpleasant, the country had become a little more undulating, enough to be interesting but not enough to be tiring, and I passed through a number of little towns and villages.

In one of these, Mt. Meridian, we stopped for lunch, and parked on a space behind a garage. A number of people came along to look at me—some schoolboys, eager and asking questions, and some men in overalls, curious in a friendly sort of way. Country people everywhere in America have a natural courtesy, a respect for the individual, which is charming. It was only in the towns that we met people in too much of a hurry to be polite.

I kept to my usual programme after lunch, walking four and running eight, and after tea felt more than usually fresh, Maury had booked us in at a motel on the outskirts of Indianapolis, some 14 or 15 miles away, and I decided to try and go the whole way. It came quite easily for once, though I didn't finish till 7.15. Maury took us out to dinner, and we drove into the centre of the city to eat at the Holiday Inn—quite a reasonable meal. In the middle of it we had to put through our call to Toronto, and when we got back to the motel there were a couple of newspaper men waiting for us. It wasn't as restful as it might have been, but we were in a capital city and had come to expect it—at least it meant clean sheets and a nice wide bed for one night.

The next morning, I ran the eight miles into the centre of Indianapolis and had a good chance to look properly at it. It wasn't a very impressive sight. If you drive into London from the south or the east you go through some poor and depressing areas, but when you reach the centre it is an imposing sight. Within a few hundred yards of the centre of Indianapolis there is visible decay—empty lots, uneven paving stones, mean streets.

Crossing the bridge over the White River, which one feels ought to be the gateway to the city, one sees rusting girders, rubble and patches of weeds. There are a few tall buildings and 'respectable' streets, and then one is back to an atmosphere of squalor again. Human beings are so much creatures of their environment that it is hardly surprising that American cities breed violence and crime.

I had a companion for several miles of my run through Indianapolis, a fair-haired young man who was keen on jogging. We talked about running and fitness, and the extra pleasure that one gets out of life from feeling fit. He was telling me how he ran two or three miles a day: 'I start out pretty easy, and then when I turn round, and only have a mile to run home I really stretch out and come home fast. It's a great feeling, beats anything I've got from drugs.'

Chapter 11
Indianapolis to Mt. Pleasant, PA

We were rather late in getting out of Indianapolis. Yet another TV station wanted to do an interview during my morning break, and we had a visitor, representing Caravans International who needed to take pictures of us inside and outside the caravan. However, we got away at last, for another twelve-mile stage before lunch, leaving Maury to busy himself in town. I did my twelve miles, we pulled into a lane just off the road and had our lunch. We had just finished when Maury came along, and having ascertained where we were, dashed back into town to put out his piece for the wire services. I sometimes felt that he was working a lot harder than I was.

In the afternoon we passed through Greenfield, where as well as the statutory reporter and photographer I had a visit from the radio station. They sent a man along to tape an interview with me, while I was on my after-lunch walk; he did this during my first mile, and then came back, full of apologies to do it all again, as his machine had not been recording. I didn't mind, but I think he got more exercise than he had bargained for. The road was quiet again on this side of Indianapolis, as Route 70 had siphoned off all the traffic; I pushed on through Charlottesville and Knightstown and as far as a hamlet called Dunreith.

The memories of all these places blend together now. As I approached each town, I would see first the signs of the petrol companies: 'Texaco Ahead', 'Gulf Station three miles', 'Enco 2½ miles, Westside of Town'. Then there would be the signs for the motels: 'Sunset Court, refrigerated, TV, 30 rooms,' 'The Blankville Motel, Pool, TV, from $6'. On the outskirts one would see the official sign on the city limits, with a little bit of information, either 'Blankville, founded 1902', 'Blankville, Pop. 1670', or 'Blankville, elevation 1,302'. I noticed that where the elevation exceeded the population, they usually put up the larger figure, unless the town had been founded before 1880, in which case it had historic significance. A few hundred yards further on would be a sign 'Welcome to Blankville', giving the days on which the Lions, the Rotary Club and the Elks had their meetings, and perhaps another giving the location of various churches and chapels. After this one came to the filling stations themselves, with the price of gas in huge figures under the sign, then to the motels, and then to the clustering of buildings which indicated the centre. I would pass the lights strung over the crossroads, and then come to the residential area, where the lawns ran down the sidewalk and the willow tree shaded the children's swing. The women and the old people would look up from the porch, and the kids would sometimes pedal along beside me, bright faces and bright questions.

There was a noticeable lack of trailer parks in that part of Indiana, but we found a roadside park just east of Knightstown which seemed to suit our purpose—it had lavatories, running water and picnic tables under the trees. We were surprised to get a visit from the State Police, who wanted to know if we were staying there for the night, when we said we were, they said they would keep an eye on the place, as there had been complaints about 'happenings' there. He didn't specify what the 'happenings' had been, but we were all agog; we had our frankfurters, beans and beer, followed by orange ice cream, and settled down to await events. At intervals through the evening men would arrive singly in cars and wait around for other men, late at night we heard cars coming and going, and once the police apparently moved somebody on. It was either being used as a meeting point for homosexuals, or possibly a distribution point for drugs, neither of which we expected to come across in this peaceful farmland.

In the morning, it was a quick rinse under the cold tap, and on to the road again. After an hour I saw another car alongside Sue's, and when I got up to them, I found I had company—the American marathon runner Ed Winnow. Seldom have I met anyone with whom I got on better. Most distance runners have the same temperament, but Ed not only knew the international running scene and most of the people in it, he also had the same educational background, being a biology graduate, doing research on physiology of exercise. It was like water to a thirsty man, to be able to talk about almost anything I chose and find somebody who knew what I was talking about.

We did about six miles together before break, and about five miles after it, before Ed and his wife Rita had to get back to their college. Sue and Rita had got on well, and as they had a five-year-old daughter; Clive too was sorry to see them go. This was the worst part of this kind of trip—as soon as you got to like a place or a person you had to move on, with little chance of ever going back. It was like being in a circus, except that circus people go back to the same places every year. After Ed and Rita had left it was not far to my lunchtime stop, which was on the west side of Richmond, Indiana. Just about the time I was due to stop, we came to a little park, set back from the road, and had a relaxed couple of hours. Clive found a stray kitten to play with. Since losing his horned toad he had adopted and lost a couple of tortoises, and if the caravan had been larger, we would have had a whole menagerie.

We played some music, I drank my coffee, and drifted away into the world of David Copperfield, Peggoty and Uriah Heep. In many ways they were more real to me than the figures who passed briefly before my eyes in these days on the road. Every day I would see things, my attention would be caught by something unusual, but the causes of these things, and the effects of actions which I saw or read about, I could only guess at. It was like seeing a very realistic film, or like travelling in a time machine, without being able to get out of the machine, nothing really happens until communication is established, until mind meets mind.

In the afternoon there was plenty of diversion—first there was the town of Richmond, then the state line, where I crossed into Ohio. It was still a nice quiet road, and in Ohio the mile markers started up again. The more ways I had of measuring my progress the quicker time passed; I timed each mile, getting faster, until I got down to 6:40, which was exactly 9 mph. My first week out of St. Louis had been scheduled to finish at Bachman, Ohio, and that evening, by running 50 miles in the day, I reached the scheduled spot. The week's run had been 335 miles instead of 324, but I was there, and in good shape. I felt pleased with myself, and we rounded off a good day by finding the best camp site of the whole trip.

As soon as we got into Ohio, we could see the signs of longer settlement. The countryside had more of that particular kind of beauty, so familiar in England, which comes from a compromise between the natural vegetation, the needs of the farmer and the inclination of the inhabitants. Thus, a hill might have a smooth green top, where woodland had been cleared for pasture, and the folds of the hill might be set off by the sharp vertical of a farmhouse or a barn. The scene was possibly beautiful because it had this familiarity, because the eye could focus on a herd of grazing cattle, a square of wheat or a dark clump of trees beside a lake, and then slide away to the soft background, where the same simple themes were played with variations which never ended yet never repeated themselves.

The camp which we had found—Imes Park—was fifty years old. A stream, of the kind in which one would expect to find trout, fell from waterfall to pool, smoothing rocks and leaving little beaches. A rocky path led up to a series of lawns, with trees, through which picnic tables and the occasional trailer were strewn. When Mark drove me up to our site, Sue was cooking supper, Clive was catching crayfish in the pools, and other children were splashing in the swimming hole. A little way up the river it was quite still, you could see the fish move, watch a dragonfly, and hear the frogs croaking, if you walked through the veil of trees that surrounded the site you could see mile after mile of farmland, warm under the evening sunshine. There was a complete peace, in which I could feel once again the size of the land. Before breakfast the next morning I plunged again into that cool river water, and started the day refreshed and at peace.

It was as well that we started in a good frame of mind, because that day we had a record number of visitors. I got the first session done quite smoothly, but in the middle of break the first TV crew came out, did an interview and took some film. I had only gone a couple of miles, through Vandalia and over the great North-South Freeway, Route 75, which runs up to Detroit, when I rounded a corner and almost fell on top of another TV car, they came along for a mile or two, filming off the back of the car, and before they had left we picked up several 'whirl-wishers' (as Clive called them). There was a fat man and his son, who jogged a few yards with me and wished me good luck, a group of boys on bicycles and a party of English people, one of whom was a distributor of the Sprite caravans in the area. They too were full of vocal encouragement, particularly one middle-aged lady, who waved her Union Jack vigorously, uttering shrill screams of enthusiasm.

Later on, the local Schweppes bottler met us, too, and took some photographs, and when we stopped for lunch on a quiet country road, everyone descended on us. We were passing due north of Dayton and Cincinnati at the time, and were only 15 miles west of Springfield, Ohio. Apart from the whirl-wishers, we had two young reporters from the Dayton paper, college students I think, who took up over 40 minutes of my lunch break asking innumerable questions. A journalist cannot be expected to work without asking questions, I know, but unless he can establish some rapport with his subject it becomes merely an interrogation. When I got going again, I was rather fed up, and didn't have a lot of time for the next reporter, an English woman working for a local paper, in Troy, I think. Before the day was out, we had one more TV car, fortunately just taking film, and a radio station car. I remember that the latter interviewer was rather surprised that I had kept on running in the rain. All afternoon the clouds had gathered, and just before tea we had a brief shower of warm heavy raindrops. Later on, it came down quite hard, which I found most refreshing, and as I approached Springfield it really started to pour.

There are, I believe, seven good-sized places called Springfield in the United States. The Ohio one is a city of 100,000 people; it appeared to me to fit in with the trend I noticed as I moved east—the advertising less brash, the houses closer together, larger and shabbier—but the sky was so gloomy and the rain so heavy that I didn't spend much time on comparative architectural studies. I made good time through the town, as good as the rush-hour traffic, but was soaked to the skin and beginning to feel cold. The water was running thickly in the gutters, and passing trucks threw solid waves of water at me. I had hoped to go on that night to Harmony, six miles out of Springfield, but on the city outskirts I found that Sue had decided on a motel for the night, and had found a good place right on the route, though it was three miles short of Harmony, I was feeling cold, tired and hungry, and seized the opportunity to stop there. I hadn't had a bath for three days, discounting my swim in the river, so appreciated the luxury of soap, a hot shower and clean dry clothes. The rain teemed down all evening, so we had supper in our room and watched TV; just over the road *Gone With the Wind* was showing in a drive-in, so Sue went to see that, while I, not feeling capable of staying up till 1 am, went to bed early and slept well.

Being in the East was less restful. The next morning started badly, as we were at odds with Maury over the fact that he had arranged for us to go on a TV show at 7 am on the morning after our arrival in New York. We had rather been hoping for a lie-in on that morning. When I set off on the road to Columbus, there was a head wind, and no shelter from the heavy tragic. The next thing was that we heard that *The Observer* had never received my previous week's despatch, the one we had given Maury to take to Terre Haute. I was particularly annoyed, because I had taken a pride in trying to produce a well-written piece every week, however tired I felt, and we had managed to get it off even when we were miles from anywhere. We never discovered why it didn't reach London, but as it was the only occasion we had asked Maury to send it off we weren't feeling very well disposed towards him for the rest of the day. He went on to Columbus, and by the time we met up again in the evening I had worked any bad temper out of my system.

I went through Brighton, Summerford, Lafayette and West Jefferson, where we stopped for lunch. We met a cheerful couple of newspaper men from Columbus, and a young man called Steve Farber, an engineering student. His father owned a garage and sold Sprite caravans, so he came out to take some pictures. He and Mark got on very well and they arranged to go out in the evening—poor old Mark's social life had been very restricted during the run.

I came into Columbus in the afternoon. As it was a Friday, the traffic was pouring out of town, and with construction work going on there were several jams, but of course these don't affect pedestrians. Sue went into the city centre right after lunch, to send off my *Observer* piece and to get her hair done, so Mark and Clive looked after me. We had tea in a park on the outskirts of town, where I was interviewed by a TV crew consisting of one man. He had driven some way with me, stopping now and again to take film, and for the interview he slung the sound recording unit over one shoulder, rested the camera on the other, had one microphone round his neck and gave the other one to me. He then drove himself back to the studio.

Columbus, which had for me always been associated with James Thurber, had some of the dignity one might expect from a city of half a million, though again there were some scruffy areas very close to the centre. I picked up three supporters here, big high school boys in t-shirts, who were very friendly and enthusiastic, but them apart, I received, mercifully, very little attention. I jogged on and on along pavements, across lights and on to more pavements, I could not find out how far it was to Reynoldsburg, where I hoped to stop that evening. I asked in the hairdressers, where Sue was waiting, and they said ten miles, then I tried a garage, and they said twelve or 15 miles.

After the shabby-looking inner city areas I came to richer, cleaner streets, and then to the motel/garage belt. Here I found that Maury had booked us in at a Howard Johnson motel, which looked very nice. Leaving the others to get themselves straight I jogged on for another half hour, and having done fifty miles, found myself in Reynoldsburg—it was only six miles from where I had asked the way. One of the Reynoldsburg signs said, 'Home of the Tomato', and on reading a notice in the centre of town I discovered that this was indeed the truth, and that the useful tomato, which I had imagined to have been with us for centuries, was in fact born and bred in that ordinary little town, less than 80 years ago. I wonder what people ate their beans in, before the coming of tomato sauce?

After a trying day, the Howard Johnson in Columbus was a restful place. Clive loved the warm indoor pool, I enjoyed a full-length bath, instead of the usual shower, and we all enjoyed dinner and breakfast in less cramped surroundings than usual. We were fond of our little caravan, it was often a welcome sight to me, but it was luxury to be able to spread out a bit.

Saturday found us once more on a quiet road, as Route 70 had once again taken the load. It was very humid, though not hot, I ran through Wagram, and Luray, Kirkersville, Linville and Brownsville, till at last I came to Zanesville. The most notable feature of the day was that it was the only occasion when we had any trouble with the cars. After the morning break the MGB would not start; this meant hitching the caravan—on to the Austin America, which we had fitted with a tow bar for just such an emergency, and then Mark and Maury towing the MGB into Zanesville. We worked out various plans for getting the trouble fixed in Wheeling, if it couldn't be done in Zanesville, but it turned out to be a minor electrical fault which was soon put right, and the Austin was able to resume its normal role. Still, it had coped all right with the caravan, in spite of some quite large hills.

As far as I was concerned, nothing much happened till we got to Zanesville. Occasionally people who had heard of my progress on the local radio would come out of their houses to take a picture and give me a wave but being a quiet road, we had very few 'whirl-wishers'. I think it was the day before that I encountered a particularly aggressive bunch of women, who had for some reason been expecting me much earlier in the day. They practically screamed at me: 'Hey, whereya bin the last three hours? We bin waiting here three hours for you. Hey, stop and talk to us.' I wasn't going to get involved with them in that mood, so I kept on running.

Prompted by this and other experiences I wrote in my *Observer* piece that week:

Like the Lord High Executioner we have our little list of types we could do without. There is the fortunately rare character in long shorts and rolled-up shirt-sleeves who says: 'I'm from Wolverhampton' and expects us to fall on his neck with tears of joy. There is the bland fattish young man in a dark suit, who after a brief enquiry proceeds to tell us about himself, his wife, his church, his college career and his general excellence. There are also aggressive middle-aged ladies, generally in pairs, with tight mouths and a good deal of excess poundage, who regard us as public property because they saw us on TV and make demands accordingly.

To be fair, the vast majority of people we meet on the road are both courteous and encouraging, but at the end of a hot summer day, when the fiftieth person leans out of the window of his air-conditioned car and says to me, with my sweat, mahogany tan and sun-bleached hair: 'Are you the guy who's jogging to New York?', I'm sorely tempted to say: 'No. I'm Ho Chi Minh!' and leave him to figure it out.

At the end of the day, while the others had gone off to find a state park marked on our map, I ran into Zanesville. The Freeway roars straight past Zanesville and has left untouched an interesting nineteenth-century town. The Muskingum River runs through its centre and is crossed by a remarkable Y-shaped bridge. On the eastern side the wooden houses climb up a steep hillside, and they lean together, as in some Alpine village. It was a long winding hill I had to climb; just before the top was a memorial and standing beside it was an old man. He said: 'Would you like a grapefruit?' I said yes, I would, so he promptly cut one in half with his clasp-knife and prepared it by scooping out the pith in the centre. As I sat on the grass and sucked at it, he told me about himself. 'These are real good Florida grapefruit. Got 'em down South. When I lived in Florida, I ate almost nothing else. Then I got arthritis. You a vegetarian? Well, I am, and I'm 75.' He looked ten years younger, his face was brown and his grip firm. He was moving north again now, driving a camper truck and taking his time. He was a lonely man, and glad to talk. After I finished the grapefruit, which was very good, we shook hands, and went our ways.

The rest had done me good, and I managed another four miles before Mark came out to collect me, making 47 or 48 for the day. It was starting to rain when he picked me up, and by the time we reached the camp it was pouring. Having found such good camp sites recently, we had gone nearly 20 miles south to find this state park, deep in the woods, but it turned out to be rather a disaster. It was Saturday night, and the woods were alive with campers, trailers, tent trailers and all the paraphernalia. Families were lighting fires, getting water, putting up awnings, and there was a rather officious Ranger with a moustache, making sure that everyone obeyed the regulations. Over the whole scene it rained steadily, dripping its way off the leaves and finding its way down the back of your neck; puddles around our door grew and united. The only thing to do was to light the gas lamp for comfort and warmth and eat as much as we felt like. After that we played snap round the little table, till everyone got quite silly and helpless with laughter, and went to bed at half past nine.

Whatever one day has brought, there is another to come, and we never knew what was going to happen. I followed Route 40 for the whole day, passing through New Concord, which had a sign saying, 'Home of John H. Glenn', and Cambridge, Ohio. There is something in me that prefers these quiet, rather shabby places, to the glamorous neon-lit cities. The country comes further into the town and the people seem more relaxed. For a young man living there it's probably boring as hell, but for the weary traveller it's fine.

A few miles beyond Cambridge Route 40 disappears, swallowed up and incorporated into the body of Route 70. For a while I followed a frontage road, which wound up and down a bit, but went in the right direction. Finally, it veered sharply away to the south leaving me stranded; rather than retrace my steps and try and find another road, I climbed over the wire fence and ran down the freeway for four miles, expecting every moment to be picked up by the Highway Patrol. When I got down to the next interchange, I encountered Route 40 again. It ran for several miles, a tarmac museum, since no signs or advertisements had been altered, I should judge, since the 1940s. There were signs advertising motels that had fallen into ruin, and smiling girls in square-shouldered dresses, advertising forgotten products.

At Hendriksburg, I crossed once more to the south of the freeway, and half a mile later Route 40 did another vanishing trick. I took a track which looked to be in the right direction, but which took me up a steep hill, and then left me there. I could hear the roar of traffic below me, so walked across some fields and clambered down the side of a cutting into the main road again. I knew that my scheduled stopping place, Morristown, was to the north of the freeway, so when I saw a road bending away in that direction, I ran towards it.

There was a big intersection construction in progress, and I had to pick my way through yards of boulders and sticky mud. As I did so, I saw Mark in the MGB driving down the hill. When he came to the bottom he stopped, and I thought he'd seen me but then the car turned around then started up the hill again. I hurried as best I could through the mud, and ran across the road, so as to get in line with his mirror, waving my arms. Mark is the kind of driver who always looks in his mirror, so happily he saw me and stopped. They had had to backtrack and make a ten-mile detour over terrible roads, then follow the freeway till they found a turning. Foreseeing that the road might be difficult, I had decided that we would stop in Morristown, so that I would have a firm rendezvous point. I ran the mile or so into the beginning of the town, which was more of a straggly village, isolated clumps of houses with empty stretches of road in between, but it was a further two miles before I saw Sue out on the road waiting for me.

Though I had come only 48 miles on the map from my morning start, I reckoned I had covered well over 50 on the ground. Maury was now in Pittsburgh, so we only had ourselves to worry about. By chance we had found a parking space behind a roadhouse, glorying in the name of The Grove Nite Club. There were several such places on the road, bearing a 1930s appearance, in which time they had enjoyed a brief heyday, before the freeway was built. Judging by what we saw, there was not much Nite Life in The Grove nowadays, and the owner supplemented his earnings by driving the school bus and by renting out space to trailers and mobile homes. There were several children there, who played with Clive; he was usually full of energy after a day of sitting in the car. This time the game was roaring down the field on a bicycle and skidding at the bottom; he also did a bit of trading of coins and stamps. After supper we all went up the road to a drive-in; Clive had been pestering us to take him to one and was going to enjoy it whatever film was on. In fact, we saw Gina Lollobrigida in *Buona Sera, Mrs Campbell*, quite unsuitable for him, but he was too taken up with the idea of watching the cinema screen in the car, and trotting off for Cokes and chocolate, to worry at all.

For some days, during our rather unremarkable progress through Ohio, I had been looking forward to the day when we should cross through

West Virginia and enter Pennsylvania. Once in Pennsylvania, I thought, the end would be in sight. Miles and maps were my obsession during those days, totalling up what was behind, working out the average and, more important, counting down the miles remaining to New York. The later it got, the less chance there was of making up any time lost through error. After several checks I noticed that I had made an error of 20 miles in the distance from New York to Columbus, which, added to my mistake over Indianapolis, brought the total distance up to 2,870 miles. I added ten miles on to each of the last two weeks, and adjusted each day by one or two miles, after that I found no more serious discrepancies. On Monday, June 6th, I set off determined to enjoy the tangible progress of crossing two state lines in one day.

As I approached the valley of the Ohio River, which forms the eastern border of the state, I witnessed a great change in the topography; the hills became higher and more dramatic, the valleys deeply cut. Down in these valleys, road and railroad wound side by side, and the smoke from the towns hung between the walls. The roads were narrow and twisty, so that it was hard to find a safe place to stop. It was a mining area, and when I came over a crest and ran along a viaduct overlooking the valley, it reminded me rather of South Wales. When we stopped for the morning break an old woman came out to say that we were on private property—the only time that this happened to us on the entire trip. As a rule, we had four long stops and eight short stops per day, and only once in those hundreds of stops did anybody get upset about our parking. If we had done the same thing in England, we would have had people on top of us all the time. There would seem to be a mathematical relationship between the degree of tolerance and the inverse of the space available to an individual.

From Bridgeport, Ohio to Wheeling, West Virginia you cross by means of two bridges and an island. Here for the first time one could feel a sense of history. The houses near the river were built on high foundations, in case the river flooded, they stood up like little islands, showing in their different styles the changes that had taken place in the valley in the past 200 years. There were the rows of houses that had perhaps belonged to miners, some fine wooden frame houses painted in their white and grey, then the black-windowed iron-framed factories and shops of 100 years ago. The iron bridge with its spans and girders spoke of painstaking struggling work by many men over a long time, striving with picks and pulleys and spanners to tie the banks together with their iron bars, while the concrete arch of the new bridge gave its simple message of twentieth-century mastery in mechanical things.

All along that road are the monuments to the early settlers who defended their farms against the Indian tribes, or, if you look at it another way, to the unavailing efforts of the Indian tribes to hold on to the lands in which they had once roamed free. I don't suppose any of them thought in those grandiose historical terms at the time; they were too busy with the daily problem of survival; it is only we tourists who try to recapture time, in order to make our own presence a little more significant.

In my case, whatever thoughts of history that I entertained as I passed through Wheeling were driven out of my head by the appalling traffic conditions on its eastern side. The roads were narrow and congested, and Mark had to take the caravan almost two miles further on than intended, into Triadelphia, before he could find a place to park for lunch. The school in Triadelphia must have been on holiday, because a lot of small boys gathered round, and Clive went out and made friends.

After lunch I walked for a while, then, attended by several of the boys on bicycles, ran on across the state line. After tea I brought the day's mileage up to 48 by reaching the outskirts of Washington, which was for the first time a few miles ahead of my revised schedule. During this last session we had to put through a call to a radio programme in London, so Sue and Maury found a phone booth and put the call through a couple of minutes before they expected me. Unfortunately, there happened to be a steep hill just before that point and, being tired at the end of the day, I decided to walk up it. Poor Sue was left talking live on the programme, trying to spin out time till I appeared around the corner; eventually they put a record on to fill in time, and to her relief I made it to the phone before the record finished.

The last few miles of the day were very hilly, but I had plenty of time and could afford to walk up the hills and jog down them. We stayed that night in the courtyard of a particularly scruffy motel, half of which had been burned down, but at least I could use the shower in Maury's room, for which everyone was grateful, as I hadn't had a good wash since leaving Springfield three days before.

The next day involved, for a change, some attention to the route on everyone's part, as we left Route 40, on which I had travelled over 500 miles from St. Louis, and made our way across to join Route 31, which ran parallel to the Pennsylvania Turnpike. The road led first through Washington, then through Eighty Four to Monongahela. It was a populous area, and every day, through Zanesville, Wheeling and Washington, we had had TV cars and newspaper men giving us their attention. Just outside Monongahela, where we stopped for lunch in a lay-by, we had yet another visit. The long red car drew up, with a friendly driver, a tough-looking cameraman full of backchat and the professional newsman, very smooth in his striped tie and trendy blazer. We cruised up and down the road a couple of times, with the driver getting used to the speed and the cameraman shooting off the tailboard.

In the house opposite a boy came out to watch, and when he saw what was going on, he went quite wild. 'Mum! Dad! Quick! It's the TV! It's the newscaster from Channel 7! Right outside our house! Come and look!' What the subject was he didn't care; it was the fact that the actual newscaster, the man who brought the world into his home, the god from the machine, was actually present in the flesh, outside his house.

Through Monongahela, over yet another broad river, of the same name, and up a series of long steep hills I went. In one place I met the Chief of Police, like a cartoon character, built like a bulldog and wearing a big peaked cap with CHIEF on it in gold letters. That night I reached Mount Pleasant, seven miles ahead of my revised schedule, and stayed in a motel nearby. It was here that Maury had arranged to meet up with a party of English people from Pittsburgh, who wanted to see me. When they turned up, instead of the twelve we expected there were two. Apparently, my piece in the previous Sunday's *Observer* had reached Pittsburgh, via the air-mail edition, that very morning, and my comments about visitors had been taken to heart! It did at least show that someone was reading the stuff.

We actually got on very well with the two who did turn up and had a good evening drinking beer in the nearest bar. All through the past week, across the plains of Indiana and Ohio, the physical side of the running had been working very well. It justified my faith in the adaptability of the human body, which can adjust itself to practically anything in time. My body was now a running machine, if you can imagine a machine which ran on cornflakes, salads, beans and Schweppes drinks. As long as I kept putting the fuel in, the miles kept coming. I was now on the last stage, with only a week's full running left, but I had been warned that the mountains ahead, the Allegheny and the Blue Ridge Mountains, were pretty tough, and if I did have any trouble there would be no time to catch up on the schedule again. I knew now that it was possible to do it, so that the sense of challenge had largely gone out of the run—it was a matter now of doing a job of work and not losing concentration, for even on the last few days a single strained ankle or over-zealous dog could turn the whole thing from a triumph into a fiasco, and with 2,500 miles behind me I didn't want that to happen.

Chapter 12
Across Pennsylvania to New Jersey

During the last week of the run, we moved further away from civilisation. Leaving Pittsburgh behind us, we did not approach any large population centres until the last three days. We had expected Pennsylvania to be urban and industrial, instead we found miles of beautiful and unspoilt country. The mountain ranges here run roughly north and south, which makes it difficult for anyone travelling from west to east, but the views made up for it. Each ridge was thickly clothed in wood land and, seemed quite impassable until one got close to it, and could see the road snaking up through the trees, or running along the valley and turning the shoulder of the hill. I suppose that the rise and fall would be about 500 feet over each range, and the distance between them about five miles. Most of the time we were at about 2,000 feet, where the air was noticeably cooler than it had been in the plains.

When you are out in the open you are particularly sensitive to small changes in temperature and humidity; you even notice changes in the flora and the insect life, thus I got the real feel of a piece of country, even though I might learn little about its human inhabitants. It is always said of the British that they talk of nothing but the weather. I suppose that if you move from your air-conditioned home to your air-conditioned office, in your air-conditioned car, then the weather doesn't matter, but in that case, you might just as well be in a coffin. For me the feel of the wind, the way the clouds move over the face of the sun is reality, it is the thing on which life on the planet depends. It was very good to be up in those hills, we had had too much of towns. From the top of one ridge you could see another beyond, and then another, and between each was a veil of moist air that changed the quality of the light and gave the Blue Ridge Mountains their name.

After leaving Mount Pleasant on the morning of Wednesday the 18th, we saw very few people. The only person who spoke to us was a Highway Patrolman, and the only clue that we were not hundreds of miles from civilisation was the dull roar of the Turnpike, a mile or two away to the north of us. We stopped for lunch a couple of miles east of Somerset and turned into a farm lane where nobody could see us. The people in Somerset had been warned that I was coming through and not only did the radio station interview me as I trotted along, but a couple of motherly-looking ladies came over and presented me with a packet of chewing gum and a tube of Lifesavers wrapped in a dollar bill.

In the afternoon the clouds came down and it rained. It was over 20 miles to the nearest town, so we camped where I finished running, in a lay-by near the hamlet of West End, this being at the western end of Bedford County. It didn't seem worth driving to a state park for the privilege of sitting under trees in the rain and, having been out in the rain all the afternoon, I didn't need a shower. I rubbed myself down and put on some dry clothes; Sue produced a hot supper and we had another old-fashioned evening, reading books and playing cards by gaslight.

I got off early the next morning, I was a few miles ahead of my schedule, less than 300 miles from New York with six-and-a-half days to go, but for some reason I felt depressed; perhaps it was the fact that although the challenge was gone, there was still a full day's work ahead of me. I started on my repertoire of mind-filling activities, but they were becoming rather threadbare by this time. The calculation of miles gone, miles to go and daily averages lasted me only a couple of miles, the thoughts of our arrival in New York and what I would do when I got back to England had been gone over so many times that their recapitulation did not last long either. I stopped and walked for a bit, until the others came past, and I could start looking forward to coffee break. We had come down from the hills into a flat valley, where a farmer and his family were picking strawberries. A little further on the valley became narrower and wooded, and under the trees was a cluster of huts and trailers, making up a little settlement, rather as if a weekend party of tourists had become enchanted there and taken root.

We took our morning break at Manns Choice, where there was a cavern, which Sue and Clive went to visit. I had to run round the end of Wills Mountain to reach Bedford, the only town on our route that day. Sue took the opportunity of doing our washing, and Mark went off to try and find some silver half dollars. I got through Bedford without attracting attention and went out on Route 30, which I was to follow for the next 150 miles.

There was a detour in operation, but I took the direct route through all the construction work. This led to a bit of misunderstanding, because Mark did not get to the end of the detour until I had already passed that point. The result was that while he was waiting for me to appear, I was speeding eastward, wondering when my lunch was going to appear. By the time he realised and caught me up, I had completed a 15-mile session.

In this area were a number of winter sports centres, and the occasional chalet, added to the wooded hills and the steep meadows gave it an Alpine appearance. As the completion of another day's run came closer, my spirits improved. At Breezewood we saw a magnificent example of American road building—Route 30 met Route 70, a freeway, at this point, and both of them crossed the Pennsylvania Turnpike. The road I was on dropped into a valley, where the interchanges went off, which was completely filled with petrol stations and motels. For miles around there was nothing but woods and farmland, and then suddenly one came to this fume-filled hollow, with the concrete posts of lamps and signs curving upwards like the stalks of some huge fungus. On the further hillside, which must have been 300 or 400 feet high, my road climbed laboriously up, then leapt with a single span the great turnpike road, which cut into the hill with a ruler-straight furrow.

On the crest of this hill, from which the chequered country below looked like a crumpled quilt, I found the caravan waiting, and beside it two cars. One contained the newspaper men who had chased me from Bedford and the other an English journalist from the *Evening News*, who had come out from New York. We had a cup of tea and a good talk, and then I went out to run the last nine miles I needed to make 48 for the day. I was back once again in thickly wooded hills, there was another detour due to construction work, again I went straight on running four miles while the others drove twelve, over very rough roads, and we arrived simultaneously at the further side.

I stopped just short of Harrisonville, where we found a really nice camp site, a new one, made in a pinewood on top of a hill, with a lake below it, where we swam, and lovely hot showers. There were camping places cut into the woods and long views. Mark and I went off to get some cans of beer, from a bar where men sat on stools in a long silent row, and then sat out drinking them till the sun went down. It was another place we were sorry to leave.

The next morning was rather a frustrating one. We had promised to put through a call to Thames Television in London, and I wasted half an hour in McConnelsburg waiting for the call to come through, before we discovered that the phone was not working properly. I then had an immense climb up Dickens Mountain, and when we stopped at a café near the top, they didn't have any ice or any milk or any soft drinks, the three things that we wanted. Of course, we had our supply of Schweppes drinks as a rule, but had temporarily run out. It grew very warm and humid that day, after several days of cool weather, and reached 90°, which with high humidity is quite uncomfortable. After that big climb out of McConnelsburg the going was mostly downhill, and I managed nine miles in an hour, as fast as anything on the trip.

We stopped for lunch just past St. Thomas, and it was there we met the English TV crew. They were filming various events in America, for ITV, and took us in as an extra. They had an enormous black, hearse-like car, that looked like something from a gangster film, but at least rolled very smoothly. We were delighted to see some English people, but from the operational point of view they didn't compare very well with the Americans. They had six people to do the job that was usually done by two Americans—a driver, a cameraman, a sound man, a boy who did nothing except wield an entirely superfluous clapperboard, a girl with a notebook and an interviewer. They took great trouble over the filming on the road, holding up miles of traffic behind them, and I expect the quality of the film was a little better as a result, but whether the importance of the subject really warranted the attention of so many experts I am inclined to doubt. At least they distracted my attention during a hot and uncomfortable afternoon, for which I am grateful.

With my attendant crew I ran through Chambersburg, which made little impression on me, as I ran round the back roads, and on to Fayetteville, where we stopped for tea. I then had another eleven miles to cover to my scheduled stopping place, seven miles west of Gettysburg. The last part of the day was routine and rather boring, running on a straight road at the bottom of a valley, with woods coming down on both sides. There were a number of motels and bars dotted along this road, and my eye was caught by one party of sportsmen. There were about half a dozen of them, wearing sports shirts which barely concealed their pot bellies and baggy shorts revealing white scrawny legs. They appeared to be making for the bar after a day's hunting, and I wondered whether these were some of the husbands of the elderly ladies we so often saw, very smartly dressed and corseted, with blue-rinsed hair so carefully arranged. We met many Americans whom we liked, but we saw too a good many who confirmed us in our prejudices by their conformity to type.

A few miles before I was due to stop, we passed the California Park, a large and popular state park on the Appalachian Trail, and there we stayed the night. During the last mile of my run I met a fellow runner, called Joe, who had driven down from New York to accompany me over the weekend. This was a great boost; for one thing it brought New York that much closer, and the prospect of having company for the next couple of days lightened the load considerably. We all went back to the park and drank a few beers, which I discovered was verboten.

The only trouble with state and federal camp sites is the vast number of rules, but I suppose these are necessary in a place where the people come from such widely different backgrounds. We discovered one of the advantages of the state parks (in addition, that is, to the dustbins, lavatories and showers) which was a film and lecture show by one of the wardens. The material was pretty elementary, the names of some of the trees and animals, and a lesson on how not to set the forest on fire, but Clive was enthralled, as he has a genuine interest in natural history. As it was a Friday evening, the camp was very full, and we were amazed at the number of adults who sat and listened to this talk for over an hour. It may have been due to the fact that they didn't have their TV sets with them, or it may have been the result of an instinct to take part in whatever is being organised, but I prefer to believe that it was due to the passion for knowledge and for self-improvement which is found all over the United States. Young, middle-aged and old people sat in solemn rows under the trees while the young warden lectured on different types of leaves, and on the way forest fires are started. I am afraid that we in our cynical European way were content to drink, talk and merely admire the forest.

From there onwards the roads along which I was running became more crowded with traffic, and the frequency of towns and villages became greater. Add to this my increasing lack of sensibility, and you will see why the last few days of the run did not, with one exception leave a deep impression in my mind. It was lucky that I had Joe to run with; he was friendly and thoughtful, with a pleasing New York Irish voice, resembling that of

Fred Flintstone more than any other I had heard. He was an enthusiastic road runner, which of course made him our friend and gave us a common topic, but he had many other sides to his character, and we discussed many contrasting features of our two countries, jogging along at a steady 8 mph. He wasn't as experienced in running all day as I was, but even though his leg was troubling him later in the day he still came with me for short stretches. Where we got on best with him was in sharing our common outlook on life, of going out to meet it, looking for challenges and not worrying too much about what other people might think. I don't think Joe would mind my saying that he was not a top-class runner, yet he would travel anywhere for a race, do his best, and enjoy it whatever the result.

The first hour's running of the day, which I did on my own, took me through historic Gettysburg. Like every English-speaking man, this name meant something to me, and I was very glad that my route took me through it, but the commercialisation of that place completely cured me of any desire to see it. For the last six miles into town the traveller is bombarded with instructions: 'See the Battlefield', 'See the Museum', 'See the Film First', 'Stay Here', 'See the Waxworks', 'Give your Child a Battlefield Meal'. The noble, familiar bearded face appeared in every conceivable association— the Lincoln Motel, the Lincoln Gas Station, the Lincoln Stores; I expected Lincoln-flavoured ice-cream. Tourism is an industry, we know, and the Civil War exercises a powerful hold over the imagination, but I would not go here to remember it. I would rather stand by a stream running over warm stones and think that once Americans in grey and Americans in blue killed each other, and the blood of them both ran down this stream and returned to the soil.

I passed through Gettysburg in the morning, and later came to New Oxford. This little town was crowded with cars and people, by reason of the annual 'flea market'. For a quarter of a mile the street was lined with stalls, each containing a load of second-hand clothes and ornaments. It was the first time that the American enthusiasm for antiques really came to my notice; during the next few days, as we passed through the older part of the country, the antique shops became so frequent that one wondered how the Colonies managed to produce so much material.

After lunch Mark did a bit of running, and he and Joe took it in turns to accompany me. We were approaching York, a sizeable town, so Maury booked us in at a motel on the eastern side. Sue and Clive went off there, to have a rest and a swim, while I did the last few miles. In West York I had an appointment with one of the TV stations, and for some reason we arranged to meet at the fire Station. I got there early, so had time for a drink and a rest, which I needed.

York has strong English links, and the town looked more like an English town than any I had seen, there were fewer billboards, and a greater uniformity of architectural style, most of it, in the centre, showing the influence of the eighteenth-century Colonial building. The shops and the banks had more dignity and permanence, which is something I think a town needs, to help its children to grow up secure and confident.

After the interview I ran on to our motel, making a 17-mile stretch without a long break, and after a bottle of ginger beer and a sticky bun I knocked off the remaining four miles for the day. This gave us a good long evening, time to swim, change and have a drink before dinner. The food was improving slightly as we moved east, and I had a good meal, finishing up with two ice-cream sundaes and some good coffee, then went to bed and watched old movies on television; at times like this I felt that things weren't too bad.

Next morning, back on the road, the final destination was another day nearer. You may have got the impression that I was mostly interested in the country and the people that we saw, but this would be a false impression. I have always been an enthusiastic runner, and in this case, enthusiasm had merged into obsession. However bad I felt, mentally or physically, the thought of giving up never came into my head, it was simply a matter of how long it was going to take me, and the 'how long' part was something that kept buzzing in my head the whole way across. Even at this stage, with three days to go, I wasn't taking anything for granted, and felt relieved to get each stage behind me; after all, it was still over 150 miles to New York, and if I got injured, 150 miles would be a very long walk.

This Sunday was a good day. I started by having a dip in the pool, then Sue and I had breakfast on our own, while Mark and Clive were still sleeping. A few miles after the start I came to the Susquehanna River, where a curiously formal bridge spanned a broad expanse of sluggish water. A light mist concealed the buildings on either bank, and a single boat gave the scene the appearance of a classical Chinese painting. The country was still in a peaceful Sunday-morning dream when I entered Lancaster

County on the further bank. As I entered the town itself, I met another runner. He worked for the local radio station, so was combining work with his Sunday training. At morning break everybody arrived. I was doing the sound interview when the Lancaster TV people turned up, and then a newspaper man. Mark and Clive caught us up, and Joe, ready for more running, then Maury, with his wife and children, who were spending the weekend with him. After we had done the interviews Joe and I started running, while Maury's family took Clive to an amusement park and Sue went on ahead.

As I left Lancaster the mist cleared away and it came out warm and sunny. Traffic began to build up, we were in what they called the Pennsylvania Dutch country. Dutch of course meaning German, which is renowned for two things: one is the richness of the soil and the other is the Amish people. Ever since the musical *Plain and Fancy* ran in New York, ten years ago, the Amish have been a major tourist attraction. Even though we had been told about them it was a strange sight to see, when a little pony trotted by pulling a covered black gig. The driver wore black clothes, a broad black hat, and a square-cut black beard, while the woman beside him, wore a black bonnet and clothes which, like those of her husband, were in the style of 1850. They trotted along through the twentieth century, on their way from farm to church, bidding good morning to their friends, looking the very picture of Victorian security and smugness. I wondered how many of those who snapped their pictures secretly envied them the simplicity of their lives, and I wondered what sort of people dwelt inside those antique costumes. I didn't have time to find out.

About noon I was accosted by a middle-aged couple in a car. To my surprise they turned out to be acquaintances of my brother's wife's parents, whom they had met on a tour of Greece. Quite by chance they had read that I was coming through Lancaster that day and had come out to look for us. They insisted on taking us out to lunch; I didn't fight the sugges-tion, and we had one of the finest meals of our tour. I won't say that it was typical—it was a Pennsylvania Dutch Smörgasbord; I suppose you could say that it was regional cooking. Incidentally all the other good meals we ate in restaurants were either Mexican, Italian, French or Chinese. In any event, it was first class both in quantity and variety. I felt more like going to sleep in the afternoon than running any further, but habit prevailed, and after I had had my afternoon tea I felt better, and managed to reach

Downingtown, my target for the night. The road was dreary, and none of the towns deserved a mention, but that evening we managed to find a gem of a camp site. We had so much enjoyed our camping out in the States that we determined to find one more camp before we got swallowed up in the metropolis, and after making enquiries we were directed up to Frank's Folly, several miles to the north; it was hard to find, but, in the phrase of the Guide Michelin, it merited a detour. Frank's Folly lies alongside Brandywine Creek, near the spot where 200 years ago the British Army secured a temporary advantage over a bunch of rebellious colonists. We found a space in the grassy meadow, under trees beside the stream.

By the time I arrived Clive had made friends with half the camp, and we soon met the Frank whose folly was commemorated in the name. He got off on the right foot by refusing to take any payment—we were his guests. He showed us where the best fishing spots were and invited us to come and see the annual village Passion Play: 'I'm playing Judas Iscariot for the seventh year running, so you know what they think of me.' He had a beer with us, and introduced some of his campers, who seemed to gather round as if to draw warmth from the glow of his personality. Most of the campers there seemed to be people who kept their trailers parked on the spot and came back every weekend. There was a happy atmosphere, partly due to all the children, but owing a lot, I suspect, to the proprietor. He was one of those natural, outgoing homespun Americans whom one finds in the pages of Steinbeck and O'Henry, but less often in real life.

That evening was the last chance we had of feeling the deep peace of the American countryside. Mark fished, Sue and I watched Clive running races and being taught how to throw a Frisbee. The smoke from the camp fires drifted up, and just after sundown the bullfrogs started. We walked up to the lake to try and see them, but all we got was the short, deep boom, again and again, like a runaway foghorn, followed by a splash and a gurgle as we got close to them. I went to sleep that night with the bullfrogs still singing their lullaby, but Mark and a friend stayed up fishing till far into the night.

The last couple of days were frankly dull. The traffic got very thick and the roads were pretty narrow. On both days I covered about 45 miles, which was well within my powers, even in the humid weather which we encountered, but which still took nearly seven hours of my time.

Soon after Downingtown I left Route 30 and took the smaller Route 202, through Norristown, Montgomeryville, Chalfont and Doylestown to Buckingham on the Monday, and on the Tuesday through New Hope, over the Delaware River into the state of New Jersey. From Lambertville, New Jersey, I followed even smaller roads up to New Brunswick, where I crossed yet another large river, the Raritan, to Highland Park, and finally arrived at a point just north of Perth Amboy and just west of Staten Island, ready to sneak into the great city by the shortest possible route on Wednesday June 25th.

During that time, we were all living in the future, making plans and arrangements for New York and England, so that only isolated incidents stand out.

The newsmen were pretty thick on the ground—one of them nearly got run down, nobly trying to stop the traffic for five seconds so that his cameraman could get a clear shot. Just outside Norristown one of them decided to try a running interview; all would have gone well if the driver of his car had been able to adjust to the speed of the running, but either by design or accident he started to accelerate steadily in the middle of the interview. Sticking to his microphone in the finest tradition of the American newsman, my companion was drawn along faster and faster, though resisting the pull bravely, in the manner of a hooked narwhal on a big game line. It was only when the vehicle started hitting four-minute mile pace and he was faced with the choice of letting go the mike or pulling the horrified cameraman off the tail of the car, that he finally gave in and staggered into the ditch, while the microphone bounced and clattered away down the tarmac, until the screaming of the cameraman brought the abandoned driver to a halt. It was the funniest thing that happened all day.

I was obsessed with getting a haircut before I arrived—the last one had been before I left England, in March. I had put it off all week and was too busy on Saturday. I set out on Monday determined to stop at the first barber I found and discovered that all members of the Pennsylvania Barber's Union are closed on Monday. I then spent some time getting directions to and looking for a non-union barber, without success, and finished up by picking one at random in New Brunswick on Tuesday afternoon. For what it's worth, I can recommend any reader who is passing through New Brunswick and needs a good clip to go to Stephen's barber shop.

On the Monday night we stayed in Doylestown. The only trailer park we could find was at the back of a mobile home park; it consisted of a patch of black cinders adjoining the laundry, between the dustbins and a rusty broken-down truck. The total effect was so depressingly squalid as to be ludicrous; it might have been the set for a Pinteresque encounter; the laundry was apparently rarely used; piles of old magazines lay about. A notice in faded red ink said: 'RULES: 1. No loitering here. 2. No dogs allowed. 3. All napkins must be rinsed by hand before putting in the machine.' Below this, another notice in the same ink said: 'For Sale, 60-key bass accordion.' Was there perhaps some sinister episode in the past, linking these two announcements? It must have been something involving the unrinsed nappies, the dogs, the 60-key accordion and possibly the washing machine as well, but one shudders to think of it.

We visited Doylestown in the evening, rather than sit in the caravan in that patch of cinders. We found a pretty place with elegant shop fronts, an open bookshop where we browsed, and a group of kids hanging around the street corner where we made a phone call. So much for the glamour of travel.

The last full day was fortunately busy; there was the problem of clearing everything out of the caravan, in which we had been living for nine weeks, so that it could be taken away the moment we arrived in New York. First, we cleared out the cars, then packed our clothes and cases into them; this left us with the residue of weeks of living, all the equipment we had bought for the caravan and the running kit with which I had been supplied at the start of the run. We divided it into a pile to be thrown out and a pile to be kept and packed the latter into a trunk and a packing case, to be sent home by sea. When we got to the motel that night, we took out the rubbish and the luggage and Sue cleaned the whole thing out. The very act of packing and clearing up prepares one mentally for a change; it gives time for the mind to adjust, so that when it is finished one feels empty, with past experience put away, waiting for fresh experiences to cross the threshold of the mind.

Chapter 13
The end of the story

I have already described our arrival in New York. It was a day that I shall never forget, memorable not so much for the events it contained as for what it signified—the successful conclusion of a lengthy undertaking. When I had finished, and I stood on the steps of City Hall, they asked me: 'How does it feel to have done this?' and I replied: 'It feels grand,' because that was what they expected of me. It was impossible then to explain in a word or two how I felt about this thing that had been an obsession to me for so long, just as it was impossible to give a snap answer to the question: 'What do you think of America?'

What did I feel? I was glad to have finished, but chiefly in a negative sense, in that I had no desire to run another 50 miles on the following day. The satisfaction of achievement itself was something that grew in me day by day. I experienced some satisfaction in completing the first day; I felt a great deal of satisfaction in arriving in Phoenix on schedule after nine days; I was very pleased to get back up to 40 miles a day after my shin soreness; and at each succeeding milestone—Amarillo, Oklahoma City, the halfway point, St. Louis, crossing each state border—I felt a little more confidence and sense of achievement. Thus, the feeling on arrival in New York was mainly relief that I had covered the last few miles without disaster.

Even this was tempered a little by a realisation at the back of my mind that the game was over. Soon I would have to go back to the complicated world of responsibilities; from the simple round of run, eat, sleep and run I had to return to the problems of day to day choice—where to go, what to do, how much to spend. I can sympathise with the situation of a man who enters a monastery, cutting away the business of having to make choices, so that his mind can rest permanently on the thing that he considers important.

Alongside these thoughts, my feelings embraced other matters; I felt a little cold standing on the steps; I felt pleased that Sue and Clive were there to share the moment with me; I felt slightly worried by the prospect of making a speech at the lunch which was just ahead—all these thoughts were in my head as I stood there on the steps. I mention them only to demonstrate that one cannot answer a question like 'How do you feel?' without simplifying to such an extent as to risk giving a false impression. One's feelings have to be itemised, referred to a particular subject, and dissociated from states of mind which may be brought about by local and temporary causes. If I now put the question to myself in another way—'What do you think you have achieved?'—then I can give some positive answers.

To start on the simplest and most mechanical terms, I had achieved the fastest time to date for the longest running course in the world. I had achieved the highest daily mileage ever for a run of this duration. My actual average was a little over 44 miles a day, as against 43 a day by Don Shepherd, but my time for the actual crossing was eight days and ten hours faster than his, because of the route which I took. More significant, I feel, is the fact that over the second half of the journey I averaged nearly 48 miles a day—my best stint was 486 miles in ten days—without running myself into a state of distress, and without losing weight. Shepherd lost 33 pounds during the run; I lost only six pounds, and that all in the first part of the run. Just after I started Dr Griffiths Pugh had expressed doubt as to whether I would be able to take in enough calories to maintain the necessary daily output of energy; I answered this query positively enough, and the evidence of this performance may prove of use to future physiologists, in calculating what sort of work rate it is possible to maintain, given suitable motivation.

This is the significant point, I feel, on the physical side, that the human body has far greater powers of endurance and adaptability than most people give it credit for. I did that run without a day's ill-health, without a day's rest and without any special diet or food supplement of any kind. What injuries I did get, I recovered from completely, so that I was fitter as a running machine at the end of the 65 days than I was when I started. Part of the credit for this must go to the manufacturers of the running shoes I wore—Adidas—and the socks—Walton's Tufsox. Everyone said to me: 'I suppose you've got sore feet!' but in fact I never suffered from so much as a blister. The other reason is simple—common sense. I kept myself clean, avoided sunburn, dressed any scratches, rested and ate regularly and generally kept in mind the need to keep my body in a state of equilibrium.

If I was thirsty, I drank; if I sweated a lot, I took salt. This applies just as much in one's normal routine as it does on a transcontinental run. If I have been sitting down all day, I got out for a run in the evening. If I have been eating or drinking a lot, then I cut down the next day. I always feel that because I am fit, I can eat more, drink more, dance more than most people, but I take care to keep the body in equilibrium over the long term.

Then there is the matter of will. Whether you call it pride, self-importance, mind-over-matter or libido, there is a part of one's personality which carries the responsibility for pushing this thing through, and if it fails to dominate the other aspects then one will not succeed. It is a kind of overdrive, which functions normally only in cases of real need, but which is strengthened by adventures such as these. The danger is that this developing side of one's nature may cause an imbalance in the whole person, but the danger is decreased merely by being aware of it. My ego has fed on fame before; I hope that now it is sated.

Being at heart a Puritan, I cannot help asking the question: 'Was it worth it?' Did it do any good to expend all this effort on an entirely useless piece of physical endeavour? Apart from the fact that I may be able to communicate my experiences to other people, I am convinced that it was justified, because of the things I learnt and because of the prolonged yet intense experience which a test of this type involves. These feelings I am sure are shared by Sue, Mark and Clive, who perhaps experienced less yet learnt more. This brings one back to the questions: 'What was it like?' and 'What was America like?' I hope that I have already answered the first of these often enough—in a word, it was hard, sometimes very hard, but I did it. Before I answer the second questions, I want to digress a little, because our experience of America did not finish with my arrival on the steps of the City Hall.

We had three days in New York, filled with activities which have no place in this story, but which gave us a good look at this phenomenal city, followed by a weekend in Connecticut, and these contrasting scenes helped us to complete our picture of the United States. In New York we stayed, at Schweppes' expense, at the Waldorf Astoria Hotel, where they make one very comfortable. It was just like the movies, being able to ring up room service for cocktails while changing for dinner, white-jacketed waiters wheeling in the breakfast—great fun for a few days, unbearably claustrophobic for any longer. But then the atmosphere of New York is enough to send any lover of space and solitude clean round the bend. Solid businessmen to whom I talked admitted that it was 'like living in a tunnel', and all said that it was only the weekends that kept them sane in the summer time. The great skyscrapers are magical as symbols—they provide the most dramatic skyline that man has created—but they are not, in that proximity, suitable dwellings for human beings. I had thought that London, Rome and Tokyo were crowded, but in comparison with the business district of New York at lunchtime, these cities are oases of calm. It is all right when the workers stay in their 50-storey towers, but when they decide to emerge simultaneously on to the 200 square yards of pavement which surrounds the building it is chaos.

New York was dirty; the skyscrapers rose from dusty streets with cracked pavements. The traffic is noisy; the heat and humidity are almost unbearable; it is still one of the more exciting places in the world to live. There seemed fewer people whom one would describe as ordinary. The rich looked richer than in London, the way-out people looked further out, and the unhappy people looked even more miserable. Every nationality crowded the streets; one could imagine if not see that fortunes, and reputations, were being won and lost. When we left, having done the things that tourists do, we were not sorry to go, but still we knew that what happens in New York matters—what other reason could there be for staying there?

Before we left New York, we visited the British Leyland Motors head office, and had an opportunity of thanking them for the support they had given us. Our Austin America and our MGB performed splendidly in a variety of conditions, for which we were most grateful, and they aroused favourable comment all the way across. I like to think that British Leyland got their money's worth, because without this kind of backing very few solo enterprises would get off the ground.

We left New York on a Friday evening, in company with a few million New Yorkers. We were lucky in having a guide to lead us through the traffic out on to the New England Throughway, otherwise we might still be there. The road construction programme was as impressive as it had been in Los Angeles, but with one difference. There is no room for further expansion, and one can foresee New York breaking down completely as a viable community, within perhaps the next 20 years—there are too many people there with too many needs. It was a marvellous relief and contrast to get up into Connecticut, where we spent the weekend as guests in several homes, including that of Commander Whitehead, the chairman of Schweppes USA.

Here we had the opportunity to see a way of life, a form of civilisation which has reached its ecological climax, that is to say, the way of life most completely adjusted to the prevailing climate. I am speaking now of a sociological climate, though of course the real climate is not without its effect on the way people live. It was without surprise that I observed that the rich and the well-to-do live in the same fashion in New England as they do in other countries. When they have wealth and confidence and time, they create beauty, within the limitations of their climate, their materials, and the talent of their craftsmen. The ambience in the 'select' parts of the New England coast is one in which an aristocrat of any age would feel at home. There is peace, carefully maintained in the face of increasing pressure on space; there is a sense of sharing in a good life. The phrase 'heirs to all the ages' is a trite one, but not untrue, when you can see a Chinese vase or an Italian painting, drink good wine in surroundings of eighteenth-century elegance, or listen to the strains of Bach as the boats skim across Long Island Sound. There is, perhaps, no major American contribution to this culture as yet, but still the flavour of life in each country is different, and the patterns gradually evolve in different directions—so far, we have country music and pancakes for breakfast.

These experiences have to be fitted into the pattern when asking the question 'What is America like?' which I will now try to answer. It is very big. It is a continent. There is a lot of space to be filled in yet. I might run through a city in one morning and then run for a week before reaching another. We are apt to think of a country as consisting of cities linked together by air routes, only an hour or two apart, but you cannot fully appreciate the difference between cities and between states unless you have seen the country which separates them, and can see the changes, sometimes gradual, sometimes abrupt, in the soil, the speech, and the patterns of activity which take place. I have been able to see and to feel these. I know that the cities are only a small part of America, and not the best part. The real America is in the small towns and the farms. In spite of the wealth, in spite of the moon landing, it is still a country of farmers. This is a sweeping generalisation and therefore can only be partially true, but it does serve as a basis for understanding what I perceived. The people who govern the country, build the rockets, create the art, are the minority;

what gives flesh to the skeleton of daily living is the manners and customs of the majority. In this case the main preoccupation is with making a living, though on a vastly different material level; the average American is as closely bound to the economic wheel as the Asian peasant. The difference is that the ties that bind them to the wheel are of their own making. As the hippie movement shows, mere survival is a small problem in the States; you need to do very little work if you only wish to stay alive. The guiding rule, the basic assumption of modern America, like Victorian England, is that work is good. It is good to make money, to educate yourself so as to earn more, to pay for your children's education so that they can earn more, having got money, it is good to spend it.

The difference I felt between Britain and the United States was that the Americans are mainly concerned with earning a living, the British with simply living; with the exceptions of the more sophisticated societies on the East and West Coasts, I felt that Americans were less concerned with the quality of the lives they lead.

This sounds like a sneer. It's not meant to be, it is simply a matter of social evolution. European society has set into patterns, whereas American society is more fluid, and may always remain so, now that distances have so little effect on communication. Americans are still expanding, there is a long way to go before the resources of that immense country are being used to the utmost, and as long as great opportunities still exist, people will strive to make the most of them, leaving less energy to be devoted to the finer points of living.

There is no doubt that the opportunities do exist. European society still has so many social strata. The voices that speak are voices of privilege and power; to reach a high position often requires a path of such labyrinthine complexity as to discourage all but a few. America has maintained her simple traditions of democracy. The road is clear for anyone to make his way to public office or to private wealth, if he is prepared to work hard enough for it. I know that there is the racial problem, that a large section of the community has much less opportunity than the rest, but I would think that the chances of success for a black boy in New York are as great as those of a boy in an elementary school in Paris, and greater than those of a boy on a farm in Yugoslavia. The thing is that the routes to success are clear for those to follow who have the talent, the ambition and the energy.

It is still the land of opportunity, and in spite of the Draft, it is still the land of the free; by this I mean economic freedom, to be able to live in almost any environment you choose, cities or solitude, tropics, deserts, mountains, swamps, forests or the rock-bound coast of Maine. Even for those who never move from their home town, the knowledge that this choice is there gives an extra dimension of freedom that is lacking in European society. If you don't like this town, what the hell, you can take a train 2,000 miles and try again. The unmistakable unity of America, which makes Americans, whether from New York or New Mexico, more like each other than like, say, Canadians or Mexicans, derives from this fluidity, this interchange and sharing of experiences. We did notice that the children seem more alike than their parents, and this must be due to the effect of television, which gives almost every American child a common cultural background, a common framework of reference on which they can hang their communication.

This common background, the voice of America, is quite different from that of any other country in the world. It has fewer formal patterns, less tradition, it is closer to the experience of the average individual than the culture of any other country that I know. This often means that it is second-rate, but when it is good it comes closer to reality than the more stylised European forms. American culture is not the voice of sophistication, it has no centuries of ideas behind it, no ghostly jury to convince. It can speak the experience direct. There is a vein of pretentiousness in ordinary life, which makes itself felt in the creation of artificial traditions—the robed high school graduation, the ladies' organisations, the pseudo-Masonic societies—but there is also the underlying common sense of the countryman. Certain things strike one as ridiculous, the shortness of elapsed history necessitates the creation of heroes from some figures whom one suspects of being less than heroic—Will Rogers, Jesse James, James Whitcomb Riley—while items 'of historic interest' include things that would not raise an eyebrow in England: the site of a minor skirmish or a church 200 years old.

The things that come through clear and true are the voices of the ordinary people who have made America and have left the record of their troubles, their efforts and their emotions. It is these that are reflected best in the songs and the films, the two forms of expression most truly American. Sometimes one catches the echo of the earlier cultures, the Indian and the Spanish, to add the dimension of time. It is interesting to notice how many romantic songs in America lament distances (you can hear the whistle blow a hundred miles), whereas in Europe they lament past time. The voices are those of working people. These were the people whom we met in the States—farmers, truck drivers, storekeepers and motel-owners. They saw us come and go, with tolerance and some interest; they wished us luck and went back to work.

At the conclusion, what memories remain most clearly? I remember a time when each day was a challenge, when at every step I felt the raw breath of experience. I can recall every one of those 65 days. How many can you recapture, dear reader, from the last 100 days, which have slipped from your fingers down the plughole of eternity? I can remember how the waves fell on the Pacific shore, and how they lapped greyly at the piers of New York. I can remember the sharp brown hills and how the storms fell upon them and sent white water tumbling down the canyons. I can remember the Rio Grande, brown and sluggish through the swamps, and noble rivers flowing between wooded hills. I remember, very well, the long road winding across the nation, and the little towns along it, where the people whose lives we touched so briefly are getting up, going to work, taking their kids to school, and working with patience and hope towards an unknown future.

Wargrave-on-Thames
September 4th, 1969

The poet Charles Hamilton Sorley, who was killed age 20 at the Battle of Loos in 1915, was also a runner and pupil at Marlborough College, where Bruce taught for 30 years. Sorley ran the same cross country routes as Bruce and his poetry had a special meaning for him.

The Song of the Ungirt Runners

We swing ungirded hips,
And lightened are our eyes,
The rain is on our lips,
We do not run for prize.
We know not whom we trust
Nor whitherward we fare,
But we run because we must
    Through the great wide air.

The waters of the seas
Are troubled as by storm.
The tempest strips the trees
And does not leave them warm.
Does the tearing tempest pause?
Do the tree-tops ask it why?
So we run without a cause
    'Neath the big bare sky.

The rain is on our lips,
We do not run for prize.
But the storm the water whips
And the wave howls to the skies.
The winds arise and strike it
And scatter it like sand,
And we run because we like it
    Through the broad bright land.

Charles Hamilton Sorley

Thanks

Bruce's family are very grateful to the many generous backers of the crowdfunding campaign which made possible the publication of this 50th Anniversary edition of *Four Million Footsteps*.

GOLD PATRONS
Jerry and Nikki Barton   Joanna Lumley

SILVER PATRONS
Ray and Margaret Auerback   Peter and Ali B-J
Sebastian Blenkov   City of Portsmouth AC   Ian Cooper
Ally Crichton   The Cutforth family   Roger and Margaret Ellis
James and Efrat Espir   Rob and Griff Fairbairn
Mark and Sarah Linsey   Dinah, Eric and Seb Schmid
John and Bernadette Schofield   Prof. Sarah Springman
Vincent and Helen Stokes   Thana, Tom and Josh
Fran Thompson   Tim and Jane   Martin Yelling

BRONZE PATRONS
Harriet Baker   Hugo Blick   Chris and Ben Brammer
Martin Brierley and Julia Warr   Christine Bunch
Graham Butler and Chris Holloway   Coemgenus   Clive Cooper
Jere Dutt   Natalia Dutt   Zeus Estrada and Bill Rodgers
Marie Everett   Lebby Eyres   Roxanne Ferguson
James and Mary Flecker   Andy Gore   Christabel Grimmer
Guy and Emma   Tom Hazelton   Ian F. Hunter   Huub and Joke
Martin and Margaret Hyman   Margaret Jorgensen
Andrew Keith   Keith and Rebecca   Mark King   Nathaniel Klein
Alphonse, Michelle and Lily de Kluyver   Chris Lewis
Nnenna Lynch   Patrick McGee   Ray and Doreen Meynink
Benedicte Mulholland   Paul A.H. Partridge   Kate Plumpton
Bethany Reilly   Richard and Beryl   Roger Robinson
Guy Russell   Rob Small   Biff Smith and Camille d'Avenas
Mark Smith   Muyang Song   Kathrine Switzer   Ben Tulloh
Brian and Gill Wallis

SUPPORTERS

Alabaster & Spragge   Justyn Barnes   Noah Barnhart

Mark and George Beardmore   Franca Berr   Charlie Bladon

Charlotte Bradshaw   Sheila Brierley   Brian Browne

Doug Bryson   Janet Buck   Brig. Gavin Bulloch   Nick Bunch

Philip Cayford   Amy, Lee, Amelia and Isaac Chalk   Daniel Chen

Sarah Christie   Raffa Cinti   Neil Cook   David Cornock

Paul Cox   Pat Cradden   Deborah Curtis and Gavin Turk

Lori De Mori   Jack Eaton   Kevin Edge   Dick Evans   Gary Evans

Matt Everitt   Andrew Fletcher   Jeremy Foot   Robert Galvin

Bryony Gough   George-Ann Gowan   Eleanor Greenwood

Rob Hadgraft   Richard Haldane   Matt Hales   The Hampel family

Jane Headland   Dave Hemery   Justina Heslop   Ron Howe

Sophie Hubble   Chris Innes-Wilson   Sheila Joel   Tim Johnston

Christopher Joseph   Alan Joslin   Andrew Keith   Clare Kellar

Eli Kennedy   Tim Kerrison   Oliver Koch   Jacqui Laing

Maureen Laing   Rupert and Judy Lane   John and Marie McGahey

Bryan McKenney   Christian McKenzie   Bruce Meloy

Karen Meynink   The Millers   Fergus Murray   Saroj Nelson

Richard and Gail Nerurkar   Dylan Netter   Nick and Maggie

Daymon Nicolson   Lorien and Andrew Nightingale   Pep Ollé

Josh Ord-Hume   Penny Padovani   Oliver Parsons   Chris Paul

Neil Perry   Nicholas Pilling   Peter Povey   Fred Price

Randy R. Reitenauer   Chris Reynolds   Bob and Michelle Rich

Isabel Rocha   Kevin Rutledge   Anastasia Albertine Sakoilska

Abhilash Sarhadi   Ali Sheppard   Jim Smith   Rob Sirett

Martin Slevin   Martin and Rosie Stevenson   Michael Strevens

Rafael Susigan   Jane Sutherland   Fiona Taylor

Sally and Don Taylor   Rosalind Thomson   S. Tilston

Ted Townsend   Anne Tulloh   Anthony Tulloh   George Walker

Mel Watman   Roger and Teresa Wheeler   William and Wendy

Claire and David Wilson   Sally Woodward Gentle   Geoff Wright

and many others

1 3 5 7 9 10 8 6 4 2

Published by

the wind in the trees
37 Penshurst Road
London E9 7DT

in association with Tulloh Books

This 50th Anniversary edition edited by Jojo Tulloh

Designed and typeset by Tim Barnes

thewindinthetrees.com

A CIP catalogue record for this book is available
from the British Library

ISBN 978 1 9161687 2 5

Printed and bound by Editoriale Bortolazzi Stei, Verona, Italy